An Evening Walk

STEPS

An

TOWARD

Evening

WISDOM

Walk

AND

GRACE

CATHLEEN L. CURRY

ave maria press
Notre Dame, Indiana

International Standard Book Number: 0-87793-678-1

Cover and text design by Katherine Robinson Coleman.

Printed and bound in the United States of America.
Library of Congress Cataloging-in-Publication Data

Curry, Cathleen L.
     An evening walk : steps toward wisdom and grace /
   Cathleen L. Curry.
             p.   cm.
    ISBN 0-87793-678-1
    1. Christian life—Catholic authors.   I. Title.
BX2350.2.C85   1999
242—dc21

                             99-23218
                             CIP

To my parents, children, friends, and teachers

who have taught me,

perhaps unknowingly,

about God's love.

And especially

to the God who has given me the grace

to act as a channel of his love

through this book.

Acknowledgments

One person alone does not write a book. Thanks to the Ave Maria Press staff and to Bob Hamma and Frank Cunningham who added, subtracted, and sorted so this book could come into being.

$\mathcal{C}$ontents

$\mathscr{I}$ntroduction

Our lives are over like a sigh,
The span of our life is seventy years—
eighty for those who are strong.

PSALM 90:9B-10

How many times have I read and prayed these words?
Last year I heard myself give a big sigh and announce
to the world at large and myself in particular:

"In a few months I will be seventy years old!"

The earth didn't shake, thunder and lightening didn't bolt from the heavens, but they might as well have done so. For all my reading of *Modern Maturity*, *Arthritis Today* and the senior section of the newspaper, the reality that I was in the winter of my life finally slid down from my head, bypassed my tongue and settled permanently in my heart.

For the next few days Psalm 90 kept poking its way into my days and nights: "A life span of seventy, eighty if you are strong!"

Reality walked beside me.

You are not immortal, Cathleen! There has never been enough time to do everything you wanted to do; now you are running out of time.

I tried arguing those thoughts out of existence:

I don't feel old! My mother died at ninety-seven, my grandmother at eighty-nine. Surely modern science can keep me healthy a lot longer than my forebears.

Being rather a practical person I couldn't go on that way too long. The next thoughts were:

How many pill bottles sit on your kitchen shelf? You may not feel old inside, but your body is growing tired. It takes you longer to get going and you are ready to quit sooner. Your fiftieth high school class reunion was last summer. Surely looking at your classmates and remembering them fifty years ago showed you something.

Panic struck.

Where did the years go? What have I done with my life?

How will I handle death?

How will I like it when I am looked at as if I were superfluous, not a contributing member of society?

How will I handle the process of dying? The pain? The suffering? Perhaps even becoming helpless and having others wait on me? A nursing home?

Then the deeper, philosophical questions:

Are you satisfied with your life? Have you done everything you wanted to do with this "span of years"? If you were to die at seventy-two, do you still want to go on just the way you are? Suppose you are "strong" as the Bible says, and you have another ten years to live. How do you want to live those years?

And deepest of all:

How does God want me to live? Am I following God's will for me in these sunset years?

⊷ ═◆═ ⊶

None of us ever really know the answer to that question for sure. However, seek answers we must. We are not new to this pursuit and in seeking answers we can turn to tried and true paths on which others have walked before us. For me the path has been the way of Benedictine spirituality.

But why the Benedictines? What in the 1500-year-old tradition of these monks and nuns appealed to me? Why, as the years passed by, did this way of living—especially this way of praying—become so important?

There are numerous reasons. I became close friends with Benedictine nuns, brothers, and priests through my work with Beginning Experience, a weekend retreat providing support for the widowed, divorced, and separated (my husband died in 1971). During that time I began visiting Benedictine monasteries and became acquainted with their spiritual way.

Then, once my children were gone from the nest, I had time to consider carefully my spiritual needs rather than just following the prescribed rituals carried from my childhood. I developed a great longing for God which led me to watch these men and women and learn more about their radical spirituality of hospitality. And their balanced life of work, study, and prayer—all accomplished with moderation—was another attraction.

The founder, Benedict, a fifth-century monk, insisted on this balanced, daily routine. To achieve it, he wrote what he called a "little rule for beginners" which still provides a fitting framework for both monastic and lay spirituality today. I found it a comfortable fit with my way of life. Reading and study had always been a necessary ingredient of each day, even while raising my children. I never wanted to quit learning. As a consequence, I thoroughly enjoyed going back to college after my younger children were in middle school.

Benedict knew the importance of work—good, hard, physical labor to balance the work of the mind and prayer. In Chapter 48 of his Rule he said: "Idleness is the enemy of the soul. . . . They are truly monks when they live by the labor of their hands." Human beings were not made to loll around, as my mother used to say. She managed to instill this maxim into her three girls. Between her German work ethic and her joy of learning, she had set a good example of balance for me.

Prayer had been a given in my Catholic upbringing. Somehow I sensed that there was a lot more to prayer than going to Mass, saying the rosary, or reciting the memorized prayers of my childhood. Learning a new way to encompass my whole relationship with God would provide enough study to last the rest of my life.

The warm welcome of visitors to the monastery made me realize genuine hospitality was an important virtue in Benedict's eyes. His emphasis on stability, fidelity, moderation, and continual conversion to Christ settled in the low spots of my psyche, filling in the holes and smoothing out my path. As my grandchildren might say: "Benedict's your bag, Grandma!" After several years of visiting a monastery in northern South Dakota, I became an oblate of St. Benedict at Blue Cloud Abbey in 1988.

Perhaps that is a new word for you—*oblate.* Oblates are Christians who associate themselves with a Benedictine community in order to enrich their lives. They do not live within the community or make solemn vows as do monks or nuns. Confirmed by a sacred rite, oblates offer themselves to God, promising to love the monastery of their affiliation in order to lead a more perfect Christian life.

Finding a practical way to follow this method in my daily life required much thought, study, and prayer. Newsletters, discussions, and a delving into the writings of holy scripture and church fathers continue to push me along the path of holiness (I hope). At the time I made my oblation as a mother, grandmother, friend, and author, I had no idea that my daily routine of prayer, this community of peers, and study of Benedict's Rule would have such a profound effect on my life. It has opened up vistas and enlarged my view of the universe.

Over the years, short visits to the monastery provided the opportunity to meet a variety of new people—lay people and ministers, farmers and doctors, office workers and retired folks, housewives, nurses, writers, and teachers—anyone who wanted to become part of the Benedictine way of life. Oblates are encouraged to read and reflect on sacred scripture and pray at least part of the Divine Office (Liturgy of the Hours) daily. Obviously, all oblates cannot pray at the monastery but our prayers from all over the world join those of the monks and nuns from wherever we live.

One of the important things in a monk's or oblate's life is *lectio divina* or holy reading. Don't let the Latin title scare you. It simply reflects its centuries-old tradition. *Lectio* is nothing like reading the daily paper to be informed or a novel by Stephen King to be entertained. Rather, holy reading, which teaches us how to listen, confines itself to the scriptures, writings from the fathers of the church, Benedict's Rule, or occasionally a current spiritual writer such as Thomas Merton, Henri Nouwen, or Frederick Buechner. (Recently I used Kathleen Norris' *The Cloister Walk* as my *lectio* for several weeks.)

According to Daniel Reese, a Benedictine from Downside, England, *lectio divina* is "reading with a difference. . . . It is a slow, meditative reading in search of a personal contact with God, rather than the mastery of an area of knowledge." The first words of the Prologue to the Rule pull us up short: "Listen carefully, my child. . . ." *Lectio divina* is a way of listening to God's word.

It has helped me overcome fear, learn to appreciate each day, and help others by example. It is out of my practice of *lectio* that the reflections in this book emerge. I share them with you in the hope that they may serve, if not as a guide, then as a starting point for your reflection on your own journey. They reflect not only what I have learned in the past, but also how I hope to live in the future, for the next ten years (perhaps even the next twenty-seven, if I live as long as my mother), but always realizing death could come any day, taking me home to the God who has loved me through this life and will continue to do so through eternity.

In *An Evening Walk* I have written just what the words of scripture and those of other writers have meant to me as I move into my seventh decade. Sometimes they inspire an understanding of earlier experiences; sometimes they show me the way I should go today. Often they encourage me to let God take care of the details of my life. Sometimes the words just slumber within me until they pop up at the appropriate time.

I have used several quotations from Benedict's Rule and other writers in my spiritual quest. Songs, movies, novels, biographies, and art work also provide a realization of God's presence in my life. There is nothing in creation that cannot remind us of God. At the basis of all this search, and truly the most important, is holy scripture. The words of inspired writers and the example of Jesus give me a foundation on which to build.

I hope *An Evening Walk* can be a companion as you continue your journey. Each of us is a unique child of God and each has our own special way of processing the word of God. More than likely you will find entirely different reflections than I have on the same scripture passage. That's fine! God has a different word for each of us, according to our needs and his plan.

Growing in our spirituality is a lifetime process. Some of us do not see this need for spiritual growth as an integral part of our life until we are older. We may regret with St. Augustine, "Too late have I loved thee, O Lord." *Chronos,* the way we on earth look at time, is not God's way of measuring our lives. Grace comes with *kairos,* the fullness of God's time, when we are ready for it. Open your hearts and allow God's love to lead you down life's path, thankful for the boundless gift which has allowed us to listen, see, and act before our lives are complete.

About *Lectio Divina*

I'm sure you have heard someone say: "Each person has a story residing within." *Lectio divina* and your own lectio on life will bring your story to the surface of your consciousness, showing how God has been and will continue to be part of your story.

Should you decide to use this technique, here is a basic outline of the process and a few hints on how to go about it. Perhaps you can even start while reading this book. Pick one of the gospels and begin by reading part of it daily.

Simplicity is the basis of this reading/meditation prayer. The word *lectio* implies four basic steps in a complete spiritual journey: *lectio, meditatio, oratio,* and *contemplatio.* With *lectio* we learn to pray step by step. Day by day we learn how to hear the still, small voice within us.

1. *Lectio* (reading): Daily reading of sacred scripture is the basis of this way of praying. Seat yourself in a comfortable position, take up the Holy Bible and bring yourself into the presence of God, asking the Holy Spirit to be with you. Choose a scripture passage and read slowly, silently, and attentively. You may find your eyes lingering on a passage, or you may have an "Ah, ha! This speaks to me. . . ." moment. Stop reading. Listen to God speaking to you. Respond to his word.

   Sometimes you will keep on reading for the whole time. If the Lord has not shown you what he wants you to hear at the end of ten minutes, you can choose a word or phrase to take with you the rest of the day. Thank the Lord for being with you and speaking with you.

2. *Meditatio* (reflection): Allow the word or phrase to resonate within you, not thinking, not speaking, just letting it become part of you. Repeating it over and over allows it to become part of the rhythm of your heart. During this time let go of all preconceived ideas and allow God to break open your heart and reform you, just as you would allow a teacher to open new ways of looking at a subject. At the same time you deepen your relationship with God, your friend. You may experience a joyous need to praise him. Follow that desire. You are moving into the next step.

3. *Oratio* (response): You are moving into a personal response to the scripture text. There are many

ways to respond to God's word: thanksgiving, praise, petition, adoration, and repentance. We need to tell God what we think and feel about this word. Be honest. If you have objections to what you have heard, voice them—out loud or through the silence within. Perhaps you might want to say: "Lord, I can't do this right now. Help me to want to do it." Sometimes I find myself repeating the words of a song, poem, or prayer. If you want to ask something of God, ask. Jesus told us: "Ask and you shall receive, seek and you shall find, knock and it will be opened to you" (Lk 11:9).

Not too long ago I went to my prayer time determined that I needed to confront one of my children with some "good" advice. In allowing myself to let go of all my predetermined suggestions, I became aware of the words in front of me: "Can you not buy two sparrows for a penny? And yet not one falls to the ground without your Father knowing . . . so there is no need to be afraid; you are worth more than many sparrows" (Mt 10:29-30).

Of course! God's word to me that day was not about sparrows. I had been convinced that I needed to spell out the route my child should follow, but God showed me differently. He asked me to trust that he would care for him, saying: "If you let go, Cathy, I will care for your child." God does not lecture, advise, or command us to obey. He opens ways for us to follow him.

4. *Contemplatio* (rest): Somewhere the words cease and we rest in stillness. We may or may not feel God's presence. It doesn't matter. We are resting in God, the ultimate yearning of our soul. Just rest in his love. Allow yourself to sit in silence. Just be there with God's word enclosed within your soul. Be content to sit. If distractions interrupt (and they will), brush them gently away; return to the word which will bring you back to silence.

At the end of your prayer time, slowly bring yourself into the present. Deliberately repeating the Our Father will help you put closure on this prayer, bringing the presence of God into the rest of your day. Remember your word from *lectio*. Repeat it to yourself over and over during the day. Make it a part of your life. *Lectio* can change us if we allow ourselves to be moved by God's word.

I can hear your questions. *What should I read? Which book of the Bible should I begin with?* Spiritual directors often encourage beginners to use the reading(s) and gospel of the daily eucharistic liturgy. One of the four gospels—Matthew, Mark, Luke, or John—is a good place to start. As you become more familiar with this form of prayer, you will expand or choose different readings.

Learning to read sacred scripture in this reflective manner doesn't happen overnight, or even in a day or week. If you are consistent, however, at the end of a month or two you will be aware that you are more relaxed. Nurturing your relationship with God for at least fifteen minutes a day will not only allow your body to rest and reduce stress but will bring a peace into your soul—a peace that passes all understanding. You are finding a new friend.

This type of prayer, like all meaningful lessons of life, is a process, not something to be mastered once and for all. We will very likely spend the rest of our lives moving on this road, each time sinking deeper and deeper into ourselves, where God is waiting for us. There is no rush, no hurry to do everything at once. We have the rest of our lives to grow in our love of God.

Do I need a special place to pray? I have set up a corner of my bedroom as a prayer space. Just as we automatically move into a prayer mode when we enter a church, a special area used only for that purpose helps us to focus on the relationship with our Creator. Sitting in the antique rocker where I spent many a night nursing and rocking my babies sets the stage for my prayer time. I have prayer books and an open bible on a table beside me. Lighting a candle. reminding me that Christ is the Light of the World, draws me into prayer. Be creative and find your own space. Just a quiet corner will be fine. Each person is unique and has their own particular way of setting the stage.

Where will I ever find time to sit and do "nothing" during my busy, stress-filled life? Rising earlier in the morning or reserving a quarter- or half-hour in the evening will help you unwind, reduce the stress from an active day and send you off to dreamland with a measure of God's peace. Again, creativity in finding the time will be the right answer for you.

How long should I pray this way? If fifteen minutes seems to be too much, begin with ten, or even five. Slowly, as the peace and quiet becomes part of you, add a few more minutes. Over a period of time awareness of God's influence on your life will bring you into a closer relationship with Jesus, your brother and friend.

Trying out a new way of doing things is always scary. We fear the unknown. Come walk with me and learn to be comfortable with *lectio divina*. It's easier—and a lot more fun—with a companion. Together we will develop a loving relationship with our Divine Friend, the God who made us.

Aging

'Tis a gift to be simple,
'tis a gift to be free,

'Tis a gift to come down
where we ought to be.

SHAKER HYMN

Aging and simplicity walk hand in hand, but oh, how I can fight it. Sometimes I can be very practical and say calmly and peacefully, "Now that I am growing older . . ." but sometimes I truly hate that phrase! It seems to involve every aspect of my life, and I want to just throw it away and scream: "Life is life—

younger, middle-age, or older—and I don't want to look at how little time is left! I want someone to walk with me, to remove the rocks on which I have been stumbling for many years and make my path to God smooth and easy!"

It's fortunate that God has a sense of humor. He just sits back and smiles. But it is a smile of compassion and unconditional love, one which says: *I'll walk with you all the way, but you have to remove those rocks yourself. I didn't even excuse my son Jesus from his cross. I will give you the grace you need, but you have to die to yourself before you can rise with me.*

This is where patience, the discipline of simplicity, comes in. It paves the way for my cross-bearing walk. I need to be aware of my compulsions, addictions and accumulations—all ways of ignoring or dismissing God. If I can learn to live just in the present moment instead of constantly living in the past or the future, the clock will lose its tyranny over my life. Peace and serenity will replace my irritation and I will feel the truth of the Shaker hymn: "'Tis a gift to be simple, 'Tis a gift to be free."

The Leading-Strings of Love

I myself taught Ephraim to walk,
I myself took them by the arm,
but they did not know that
I was the one caring for them,
that I was leading them with human ties,
with leading-strings of love. . . .

HOSEA 11:3-4A

I have been working on a photo album, putting my childhood pictures in more-or-less chronological order. I found myself reflecting on these words of the prophet, Hosea: *I was the one caring for them. . . . I was leading them with human ties, with leading-strings of love. . . .*

I could see my Dad and Mother, my Grandpa and Grandma, and three aunts who lived next door bending over saying "Come, Cathleen, let go and walk to me." Those human ties were using the *leading-strings of love* to encourage and help me risk taking that first step even as they knew I would have many falls before I would be proficient. And I—I did not know that God was using those people to help me start on life's path. It took many years before I became aware that God used—and still uses—other people to guide me.

Very often it was my parents or close relatives, but there were also friends of the family, neighbors, and teachers who were important guides as I grew older. Today I find one of my children is often my instructor or mentor, helping me understand today's world, a complete turn-around from the world in which I grew up.

Sometimes I get tired of having to change. I dig in my heels and say, "No more!" Usually a good night's sleep—or even a nap—can give me the energy to take a second look. Almost always I bring the topic to God in prayer, asking for his advice. Frequently I end up agreeing that this change would be beneficial, but sometimes I don't. If the change does not agree with my value system, if it points me away from the God who loves me, then I am comfortable with my refusal.

The "leading-strings of love" come from unexpected sources. I only have to remain open to the God of Surprises and let him show me the way.

$\mathcal{D}$ry Bones

> The hand of the Lord came upon me, and
> he led me out in the spirit of the Lord
> and set me in the center of the plain,
> which was now filled with bones. He
> made me walk among them in every
> direction so that I saw how many they
> were on the surface of the plain. How
> dry they were!

EZEKIEL 37:1-2

I read this portion of Ezekiel just before Halloween.
Somehow it seemed appropriate, not only for *el dia de
los espiritus* on October 31, but for *el dia de los santos*,
All Saints' Day, on November 1 and *el dia de las almas*,
All Souls' Day, on November 2. Meditating on this, I

walked with Jesus onto the plain which was now filled with displaced bones from infants, children, mothers, fathers, and grandparents from centuries untold. As I walked among the bones I knew mine would be there someday.

Then a clattering sound began as the bones came together according to the Lord's command. But coming toward me were those of Art and Loretta, my father and mother, Sheila and Mary, my two sisters. There were bones of Katie, Nick, Rosaltha, and Jerry, my grandparents; my great-grandparents, Margaret, John, George, and Anna Frances. A little farther off were those of my extended family: uncles, aunts, and cousins two and three generations removed. Ancestors from Ireland, England, Spain, Germany, Luxembourg, and America.

But who were those others moving toward me too? They weren't related by blood but there were so many coming that the whole plain seemed to be moving toward me. Family friends, personal friends, teachers, librarians, employers, neighbors, classmates I played with and those I avoided, coworkers, lovers, even strangers. The whole plain of bones rattled and shook as they came together, all the time walking toward me.

I stood beside the Lord and smiled. They had lived and died and passed on their legacy to me. It had taken more than a village to raise this child. I stood on the shoulders of generations of human beings who made me the unique person I am today.

Gratitude flooded my soul. God's breath had enlivened those bones to tell me the story of my life. It didn't matter if I hadn't paid attention to their tales as a child or young adult. Now I understood. If I really wanted to know the details of their lives I could read the history of their times, other people's biographies and know, deep in my heart, their good (and bad) qualities, their solutions for life's problems, the values they held in their hearts and the ones they chose to uphold in their lives. Good and bad, they were part of me and I was grateful.

Those dry bones some day will dance with me.

$\mathcal{L}$ooking Back

"Truly, God was in this place
and I, I did not know."

GENESIS 28:16

It took Jacob many years of adulthood, a scheme which disinherited his brother Esau, an almost completed journey to a new country, and a dream before he realized that God had been with him all that time. Jacob had never been alone; he just hadn't recognized God's presence. Not until he looked back on his life was he aware that God had walked with and even carried him through those years. Jacob's stay in a foreign land was not only an escape from Esau's anger, but a time to learn that love can conquer resentment.

Later God told his friend, Moses, the same thing as he was leading the Israelites out of Egypt.

"When my glory passes I will set you in the hollow of the rock and will cover you with my hand until I have passed by. Then I will remove my hand, so that you may see my back, but my face is not to be seen" (Ex 33:22-23).

At those times that God is guiding and helping us, we cannot see him. We can only look back on our life and realize that he has been there, showing us the way.

That surely was true for me after Jim died. I thought I was doing it on my own, but I couldn't have been more wrong. First I began to see all the help I received from relatives, friends, and people of my community. My church and those who lived in my town were the bridge that helped me over the troubled waters of that time.

Eventually I made the connection that those people were acting as God's disciples, and, as Mary said in her Magnificat, "the dawn from on high" broke upon me. God cared very much about me and my family. He had walked with me and eased the pain, healing my soul. Looking back taught me to understand God's presence, revealing to me that even today—whether or not I am aware of it, His unconditional love supports me.

How has God carried you?

$\mathcal{W}$restling With God

> *Then some man wrestled with him until the break of dawn. When the man saw that he could not prevail over him, he struck Jacob's hip at its socket, so that the hip socket was wrenched as they wrestled. . . . Jacob's hip socket was struck at the sciatic muscle.*

GENESIS 32:25B-26, 33B

Sometimes it takes years to be able to understand the meaning of a certain Bible passage, at least as far as my life is concerned. In her book *The Song of the Seed*

Macrina Wiederkehr asks: "Are you wrestling with God?" And my answer was: *I surely am!*

Keeping control of my life had been a prime priority for me since my husband's death. Going through the stages of grief, I determined the only way to deal with the pain was to take control and run the family by myself. I gritted my teeth and plunged ahead, organizing, making work lists for the children and endless lists of things I needed to do. I counted on a routine to keep me sane.

But the children grew up, left for college, and began to live their own lives apart from me. Control was such an integral part of my life that I began to take on more and more activities to keep myself busy. But my over-programming wreaked havoc with my physical well-being and stress wore me down. I was not in control. I had a lesson to learn and, as is often the case, I was an unwilling student.

I had forgotten—if I ever knew—that my control was only an illusion. God had created us to be his children. Our heavenly Parent guides us in the way that is best for us, but I thought I was a responsible adult ready to make every decision according to my wishes. Truly, like Jacob, I was wrestling with God.

Like Jacob, God showed me the futility of my method in the only way I could understand: with a pain which originated in my hip and ran all the way down my leg. God surely caught my attention with what the doctors diagnosed as sciatica. I hurt when I stood still; I hurt when I lay down. I could sit with my leg up on a footstool, but the inactivity nearly drove me wild. Pain killers, epidural floods, and laying flat in the hospital provided no relief. Orthopedists did not recommend surgery.

With all this forced rest I began to pray, not only for the alleviation of the pain, but actually to ask God what he was trying to show me. I prayed: *Lord, what would you have me do?* And the word came. *Slow down. Simplify. Enjoy today; don't worry about tomorrow. Remember how to play. Re-create yourself through recreation. Let go of your children. I will watch over them.*

What a daunting list! A complete change was required, but one which moved in small, experimental steps to find the right way. If my first change did not work, then I needed to try a new way. At the same time, I besieged heaven to help me find God's will out of all this confusion. Slowly I found myself letting go of my previous compulsion to control, yet taking charge of the practical effort which modern medicine recommended as I grew older.

I still find myself wrestling with God over certain events in my life, but it doesn't take me long to be aware of this futile battle. It is not a giving-in to an all-powerful Being. It is an acceptance that my Creator knows the right way for me to travel, a way that will bring me closer to the all-consuming Love for which I search. What I need is a balance between helping my children at times and allowing them to make and live with their own decisions. It is a balance between control of "my" way and acceptance of God's way. Trust, faith, hope—all these lie buried deep within. They surface if I take time to listen and love. God had taken my grief, fears, sorrow, sins, mistakes, and upsets to show me a new path to follow. Sciatica had been the signpost which pointed me toward serenity in the last years of my life. God had pressed his finger on my hip so I would always be aware of his touch in my life.

Actually, it took years for me to learn this new lesson. But with my prayers and gentle reminders I ask, *What would Jesus do?* I found a delight in the simple enjoyment of the present moment, an inner sunshine on grey days. I learned the "bad" things in life did "have a silver lining" as my grandmother used to say. I learned to appreciate the rainbow and the falling star, the perfection of one rose, the complete joy and trust in a baby's smile, or the stunning work of a master artist.

Like Clara Claiforne Park, I found:

The experience we did not choose,
which we would have given anything to
    avoid,
has made us different, has made us better.

South Dakota Roots

The horizon leans forward,
Offering you space to place new steps
    of change.
Here, on the pulse of this fine day
You may have the courage
To look up and out upon me, the
Rock, the River, the Tree, your country.

MAYA ANGELOU

Maya Angelou's poem may be titled "On the Pulse of the Morning," but to me it will always be "A Rock, a River, a Tree." Angelou speaks of our ties to the land and the people who live on that land. It doesn't matter where in the world we live, what kind of terrain or soil sustains us—mountains, beaches, high plains, river bottoms, coastal plains, prairies, deserts, green oases, or swamps. It doesn't matter whether we live near the Missouri and Sioux Rivers (as I do), the Columbia, the Severn, the Rhine, the Amazon, the Danube, the Rio Grande, or the mighty Father of the Waters, the Mississippi. The very earth on which we plant our feet, the rivers, the trees, and the rocks—truly all of God's creation—influences our spirituality.

The indigenous trees of our country vary from oaks, maples, pines, and sycamores on the east coast, to the southern pines, spreading oaks, and magnolias in the deep south. The west treasures its mountain pine, golden aspen, blue spruce, and fir while the people of South Dakota plant shelter belts containing ash, hackberry, Russian olives, fir, spruce, and walnut. If by chance one is lucky enough, or faithful enough in watering, Dakotans will brag about their one colorful maple or deep rooted oak, knowing from experience how difficult it is for these slow-growing, hardwood trees to flourish in this open country. Trees speak to the steadfastness and persistence needed for our forebears to survive in this land, qualities which I hope I have inherited.

Most of extreme southeast South Dakota residents today do not give much thought to the importance of rocks in our life. My town sits on old Missouri River bottom land and any rocks in the area are usually brought in for landscaping purposes. When I joined a rock club in a nearby town, local residents thought I was referring to rock music! Yet rocks (and their absence) are also part of my spirituality. I have brought my rock and crystal collection to my new, smaller home, a foundation on which to build my changing life.

From this rock-firm foundation my spirit expands to fill the sky, which at first glance seems empty. I can agree with Willa Cather, in *The Song of the Lark*, as she describes the Great Plains: "The mere absence of rocks gave the soil a kind of amiability and generosity, and the absence of natural boundaries gave the spirit a wider range."

The prairie also has its share of dark days with storms sweeping in from the west and the south causing us to seek shelter from the elements, often accompanied spiritually by a dark night of the soul. Patience, steadfastness, and ultimate trust are needed to weather both kinds of storms.

Maybe the ultimate faith in Dakota is to believe that our God, in this land with its wide, terrible, vengeful sky bringing hail, tornadoes, blizzards, and dust storms with disturbing regularity, is also a God of love and compassion, a God who cries with us when our firstborn dies, who walks with us when hail wipes out a year's work in five minutes, who reaffirms His faith in us by giving us spectacular sunsets of gold and blazing red.

Kathleen Norris, in her book *Dakota: A Spiritual Geography*, quotes St. Hilary: "Everything that seems empty is full of the angels of God."

Living on the edge of the western cornbelt, my horizon leans forward. As I turn to the west, South Dakota offers me "space to place new steps of change" and I find the skies "full of the angels of God." I find the courage to try new avenues, to risk new ways, knowing that the God who sustains my every breath is guiding me to new vistas and new challenges.

Rocks

Trust in the Lord forever!
For the Lord is an eternal Rock.

ISAIAH 26:4

Rocks have held a particular fascination for me ever since I inherited my grandmother's rock collection, so it was only natural that I saw God as a solid rock, as heavy and stable as the piece of petrified wood in my front yard. When my husband died and my children were still very young, stability was essential for my healing. I needed a God who, with a firm foundation, would always be there to steady my faltering footsteps.

But of course we change as we age. I haven't let go of that Rock of Ages that provides steady balance to my life, but my description of *trust* has expanded. It now includes faith, not only in God, but also in myself and others. Basically, learning to have confidence in myself was the hardest part of my ongoing lessons. When I was a child I quickly learned to do only what I was told and not venture out with my own ideas. I never got into trouble if I followed orders. Some of that comes from being the oldest child. *"Everyone will love me if I do what they say."* The lesson was reinforced by teachers' discipline and society's unspoken rules. Many years passed before I could give myself permission to be creative, to speak out when I had a different idea, or even to question those I thought had authority over me.

Over the years the image of God as Rock, the foundation of life, matures into one which not only symbolizes stability and rootedness, but displays the myriad forms of beauty and inspiration with which our Creator has endowed the earth. We learn to see God, not only as a solid, immutable piece of granite or dolomite, but also as a variety of crystals or a combination of minerals: amethysts imbedded in a round geode, a swirl of silver or a quartz crystal pointing sharply toward the heavens. Sometimes I have been fooled by pyrite, fool's gold, but even then I have been able to see God's hand in that portion of his creation. My collection of calcite crystals, the most common element on earth, reminds me that even with the same basic elements, people too are different in form, color, location, and direction.

Out of this new image has also come a realization that God is so much more than I could ever imagine. He is more than the judge and record keeper of my childhood; he is more than a beautiful painting, sculpture, or building. He is found not only in every created being, but also in my relationships with others. The meaning of the old catechism answer, "God is everywhere," has expanded to have no beginning or end. My awareness of these moments—be it of a friend or enemy, book, movie or TV, computer, or even an "ah, ha!" reaction—is a daily blessing, God's gift of grace. His enveloping love continues to enlarge my universe.

The Rock of My Heart

*God is the rock of my heart,
my portion forever.*

PSALM 73:26B

I try to visualize you as a rock, Lord, but my mind moves from one image to another. I saw you as a heavy white calcite rock like the one I have in my dining room, with rounded depressions that would serve as a cave to shelter me in the storms of life.

Then I realized those storms would dissolve the calcite, so I saw you as a large outcrop of giant quartz crystals which no rainstorm could carry away. Storms would only make it smooth and shiny. But that image was too gaudy. You do not appear to me in a shining light for all to see. You appear in the ordinary, everyday life in the poor and unobtrusive, in the gentle whisper of the wind.

So I saw you next as a granite boulder on the top of a mountain. There, like "The Old Man of the Mountain" in New Hampshire, you protect and shelter me in your caves, helping me to climb higher by showing me the safe footholds and handholds as I move upwards.

Perhaps I still have it all wrong! Perhaps you are all of the rocks—and none of them! No image can encompass you. I am grateful for all you are, all the glimpses I have of your presence in my life.

$\mathscr{G}$rey Days

*Two of (the disciples) that same day were
making their way to a village named
Emmaus seven miles distant from
Jerusalem, discussing as they went all that
had happened. In the course of their
lively exchange, Jesus approached and
began to walk along with them. . . . He
said to them, "What are you discussing
as you go your way?" They halted in
distress. . . .*

LUKE 24:13-17

Today was supposed to be a day of encouragement,
of "getting things done." After morning eucharist I

had the whole day free: to write, to balance my checkbook, to clean my office, to cook myself a good, hot meal for supper, perhaps even to take an afternoon nap. Then why do I feel down this evening, as if I have wasted my whole day?

Blame it on hormones (or the lack thereof), the grey skies that are threatening snow, the phone call that says a friend is dying, the morning news that a Mideast dictator is threatening our country, or whatever you want to pick out from the avalanche of information that is overloading my psyche today. I had no trouble finding a whole list of things that went wrong. My writing was a mess. I tossed today's work in the wastebasket. I tried to write a query letter to a publisher and tossed that too. Even the article I was going to send to them looked stale and not worth the postage. I began a Christmas letter to my friends and declared it to be flat and uninteresting. Couldn't even get my computer software to set up the letter program correctly. I gave up.

I sat down to read a novel when nothing else was going right and ended up unable to put it down. It was an escape from everything else in my life.

Jesus was far away and I informed my journal I would only celebrate when Jesus was with me again. Those disciples on the way to Emmaus had nothing on me. "Distress" was a mild way of putting it.

It must have been God's grace that sent me to my prayer corner to calm down. It surely wasn't anything I did by myself. Five minutes of letting go, of

—

"breathing in the Spirit, breathing out the garbage" brought me back to my senses. It was that old bug-a-boo, control. I was trying to fix my life all by myself.

But I stuck with my breathing routine. Before long I could "breathe in the Spirit, breathe out to the world." I had let go of my own agenda and used this prayer time to ask God to help others. The focus was off myself. The "cure" was to reach out to others. My grey day had turned sunny. As Joan Chittister has written: "We are never alone in times of stress—We are simply called to recognize the mystery in it."

Simplicity

Simplicity is a process of waiting,
an ability to surrender,
a willingness to receive.

MURRAY BODO, OFM

I first began to simplify my life—at least think about it—almost twenty years ago when I heard the writer and poet, Father Murray Bodo, OFM and Dr. Kenneth Bolding, a noted writer and philosopher, lead an all-day seminar on *Simple Living*. At that time my life was anything but simple. I was going to school full time to complete my theology degree, I still had two children in grade school and three in college, and I was helping to organize a Beginning Experience group in the Sioux City diocese.

Yet part of me yearned for the peacefulness that simplicity would bring into my life. Bodo and Boulding were people of wisdom who had learned how to hear God's call to simplicity, Their words were the impetus to begin that "letting go" period of my life. God always sees what we need and brings the right gift if we are open enough to accept it. What I learned from those two men was the starting point of my journey toward simple living.

Within five years my vow to eliminate the excess "things" from my life resulted in my moving from the ten-room home so necessary for a large family to a smaller place, more suited to a woman who would be alone within a year or so. Deciding which things to take with me and which to give to my children, which ones to earmark for a garage sale and which ones to give to Goodwill showed me the latest gadget and newest style had assumed an importance way beyond necessity. I had given lip service to my "belief" that God was the most important thing in my life, but my actions showed I was deluding myself.

Simplicity is a lot more than getting rid of the excess "things" in life; excessive activities (even for worthy organizations) can replace the need for the newest model of car, boat, or computer, the fanciest house, and the most exotic vacation.

As my children left home for college and the workaday world, the gift of silence manifested itself in the house where no teenagers bounced in and out and the telephone rang only for mother. It didn't stay that way. Once the children were gone every organization in town seemed to think I had nothing to do. It took many months for me to get up the courage to say "No" to some of the requests for help. An interim step was to teach myself to say, "I'll think about it and call you back in a couple of days." Giving thought and prayer to the project was again a step to simplicity.

Time for peace and quiet has to be built into our lives in order to be open to love. Murray Bodo says silence is waiting, being present to one another, an ability to live in solitude, listening to God's word. I must be able to truly say: "The Lord has come into my life and loved me."

This is not as easy as it sounds. The walls which I built to protect myself had to come tumbling down, one brick at a time. Noise, chatter, rushing to work or home for the family, watching the mindless programs on TV, or reading one romance novel after another had to be cut back or dropped. The false premise that helping people is more important than making time to see what God was asking me to do had to fall by the wayside.

I don't automatically know God's will; I have to listen to that still, small whisper, consider how much energy I have, and pray I am making the right decision. Sometimes my idea of God's will turns out to be wrong. Then I have to say: "This isn't right. I have to try again." Always though I learn something through the choices I have made.

The Shakers had it right: simplicity is a gift. One of God's most important gifts has been the creativity to bring simplicity into my life. God's gift of simplicity has come to me in a very slow stream, not like a birthday party where I open all my gifts in one day.

Worry

> "Look at the birds in the sky. They do not
> sow or reap, or gather into barns; yet
> your heavenly Father feeds them. Are not
> you worth much more than they are?"

MATTHEW 6:26

Worry, worry, worry! How we fuss about tomorrow,
or the day after, or somewhere deep into the future! I
remember my mother being a worrier, although she
always denied she was. I remember my saying: *I will
never be like that!* Ha! I think worry was bred into my
genes.

Yet when I read scripture where Jesus talks about his Father's love and care of each one of us, I know that I am being asked to let go of this anxiety and trust that he will care for me. I look back on my life and see how God has been with me all those years I was raising the family, steering me back into the right path when I strayed. Why would I think he would leave me now?

He won't. The story of the disciples as they tried to row across the Sea of Galilee during a storm (Mt 14:22-33) is another reminder of how I need to trust. They were a group of frightened men. Jesus walked across the water and got into the boat with them. When he turned to the storm and rebuked it, the wind calmed down and all was still. We need to trust that Jesus will get into our boat and calm down our storms too. "I believe, Lord; help my unbelief."

The Prayer of Suffering

I have seen the misery of my
people. I am aware of their
sufferings and I have come
down to rescue them.

EXODUS 3:7-8

You are hurting and you don't want to hurt. Your body aches, the tears flow, and you want to run the other direction to get away from the pain—be it physical or emotional.

Take a look at the crucifix. Jesus suffered, hurt, and surely cried at the pain he felt. Your suffering and loss is part of his suffering and loss. You are sharing in his redemptive work.

William Johnston in his book *Being in Love* says that when suffering comes, don't try to find some particular method of prayer. If you have a routine or ritual that you follow, let it go for the time being. Just be with the Lord in your suffering and join it with his. Just sit and accept your cross. The Holy Spirit is giving you the way. Just sit and accept totally your hurt, anguish, and pain. This is your prayer for today.

It is easy to say this and easy to write about it, but the actual doing is very painful. Human nature demands that we run from or ignore anything that hurts us, whether it is physical or emotional. We beg God to take away this gnawing pain and when that doesn't happen, anger is likely to flare up.

Remembering that anger is one of the first stages of grief can put our suffering in a whole new perspective. When we hurt, we grieve. We have been through denial, now we alternate between anger, bargaining (begging God to change his plan), and depression (anger turned in on ourselves). It requires a leap of faith to believe that fully facing our hurt, fully accepting our life just the way it is right now will bring healing.

This prayer is not words or thoughts. You might almost say this prayer is not tangible. It is the actual letting-go of our preconceived ideas of what prayer is. It is total acceptance of your life and your cross. Jesus must have prayed this type of prayer in the garden at Gethsemene the night before he died. It was there he found the strength to go to his death the next day. This is where we too will find our strength to go on when our losses, loneliness, pain, and suffering are almost too much to bear.

If a person is causing your suffering, accept them for who they are (or were) just as God accepts and loves you. The *feeling* of acceptance and love may not come right away; the letting-go may have to be done over and over again. But each time we do this, the Holy Spirit takes our prayer and lays it at the feet of the Father. We only need to *sit, be, accept,* and *love.* That is enough. Healing will come in the fullness of time.

Comfort

*Meanwhile, the disciples urged
him, "Rabbi, eat." But he said
to them, "I have food to eat
of which you do not know."*

JOHN 4:31-32

It always surprises me that a certain passage of the
Bible strikes home when I am meditating in *lectio*.
Finding this passage in the story of the Samaritan
woman at Jacob's well, I smiled. Being available, listening, giving hope, and preaching the Good News is
the food Jesus spoke of to his disciples.

A soothing bowl of oatmeal and raisins, a chocolate bar, or bowl of ice cream can be a great source of comfort to me when worried, depressed, or overwhelmed, paving over my anxieties and letting me think all is well. Recently I noticed I don't need comfort foods if I have someone else in the house with me. When the children and grandchildren visit, a friend drops in, someone calls to talk, or even if I receive a good letter in the mail I am energized and I forget my aching bones, my tiredness, or depression. This bond with others gives me the deep joy that other times I try (and fail) to find in food.

I live alone and I must admit, I like it. On the other hand, food never tastes as good as when I have someone across the table from me. I can't go very long without the companionship of those I love, friends who are traveling on the same journey through life and those who share the same interests. There are opposites within me that need to be reconciled. Louis Auchinloss refers to it as the "dichotomy of the one and the many."

Perhaps there is a solution to this. A small voice says: "Why not spend one or two minutes visualizing Jesus as your meal companion before you eat?" And I nod my head, knowing I need to find new ways to adapt as I get older. *I have food to eat of which you do not know.*

Remembering this insight from Jesus' life can be the path that helps me to drop my "comfort food" and instead find comfort in Jesus.

$\mathcal{L}$etting Go

> "Our Father in heaven
> hallowed be your name,
> your kingdom come,
> your will be done
> on earth. . . ."

MATTHEW 6:9-10

How many times I have said *"Your will be done."* But today, when someone in deep grief called me, my first reaction was to give advice. After all, hadn't I written two books on how to handle grief? Wasn't I "The Expert"?

As I settled back in my chair to listen, I silently whispered to God: "Let me be your channel, not my ideas but yours." I don't remember anything I said, but just the calmness and peacefulness that entered my soul seemed to extend to the caller and we were able to listen and truly hear what the other said. More importantly I was able to voice my truth and show her different ways of looking at the occasion of grief. Surely God's presence was on that telephone line with us. *Amazing Grace*, indeed!

On Giving Drinks

When the Well Is Dry

When a Samaritan woman came to draw water,
Jesus said to her, "Give me a drink." . . .
The Samaritan woman said to him, "You are a Jew.
How can you ask me, a Samaritan and a woman,
for a drink?" Jesus replied:

> "If only you recognized God's gift,
> and who it is that is asking you for a
> drink, you would have asked him instead,
> and he would have given you
> living water."

JOHN 4:7-10

Sometimes I get tired of walking with those who
are hurting, giving a drink of water to the thirsty,
comforting those who mourn, listening to other

people's pain and questions about the meaning of life. There are days, or weeks, or months that everyone comes to me asking for help. No one realizes that I have needs also; no one is able to give me comfort. I say, *I can't give any more. There is nothing more within me to give. My well is empty.*

Ordinarily when this happens I know it is time to retreat someplace that has solitude and silence and just get away from all outside chaos. Often I go to the monastery. The peacefulness, the calmness, the presence of God in the monks refreshes my soul and I am able to come back with my well filled with living water.

But sometimes I can't take a few days to leave my home and find God in the monastery. Those are the days I have to find him in the bits and pieces of time that my daily life allows me. That is when this scripture story from John fills up my well.

Jesus promised the woman at the well that all she had to do was to ask for the living water and he would give it to her. I take that thought with me as I retreat to my bedroom and just let go of all the worries, anxieties, pain, and sorrow that are filling up my soul. Usually the tears flow, and I just allow them to come. I tell God of everything that is bothering me, even though I am sure he already knows exactly how I feel. He also knows how good it is psychologically for me to express those feelings in words and not leave them bouncing around inside me. Even better is writing those feelings down in a journal. There is something about getting those thoughts out of my head, down in black and white on a sheet of paper, that removes them from the awful cycle of worry in my brain.

I especially include all the anger I am feeling—anger that I may have a hard time admitting. For instance, you might want to tell God of your anger at him for allowing your mother to get this awful cancer, your anger at the doctor who showed no sensitivity to her when he pronounced the diagnosis, at your brothers and sisters who are not able to give you any help, your grandma who has a whole list of needs of her own, and your Aunt Mary who is no help to anyone! Putting your feelings down on paper will bring up some surprises. Once you get writing you never know what your subconscious will produce!

When the tears have stopped flowing and a measure of calmness and peace has descended, I spend fifteen to twenty minutes meditating on this story of the woman at the well (John 4:1-42). I tell Jesus I want this living water in my well—not only to help me, but to have some to give to others who pass by this way. I spend a few minutes relaxing my whole body—from the tip of my toes to the top of my head, letting go of the tension and stress which has built up inside me. Then I sit and listen to what Jesus says to me, as I stop at the well with my pitcher.

If worries, anxieties, or fleeting thoughts rush to the forefront of my mind (and they do), I just gently brush them aside and return myself to the well. If you spend fifteen to twenty minutes like this you will come away with your well filled up. Jesus doesn't fail us.

Solitude vs. Social Life

Solitude is . . . the place where the emergence of the new man and the new woman occurs.

HENRI J. M. NOUWEN

Where does a young girl go to flee from the authority figures in her life? Where does she go to be by herself? To be free of bossy adults who always find some job for her or inform her that "a lady doesn't act like that, Cathleen!"

In the wintertime my upstairs bedroom was a place of refuge, complete with the latest pile of books from the Carnegie Public Library. Lying flat on my stomach across the bed I withdrew into the worlds of Nancy Drew, Heidi, Beauty and the Beast, Greek gods, Pearl Buck, Richard Halliburton, and Fu Manchu.

In the spring and summer my favorite retreat was the ancient, gnarled apple tree in our back yard. The branches filled with blossoms or tiny green apples beckoned a child with a book and I spent many an hour traveling around the world with my favorite authors. To this day, when the "shoulds" of my life are overwhelming, I will often retreat into a good romance novel and withdraw from the reality of making decisions. Those tried and true solutions from my childhood are difficult to change! Perhaps change isn't necessary. Stories provide a needed retreat from hasty conclusions, providing a back-off space to look at the problem from a different perspective.

A trip down memory lane brings up those adults and peers who, with their interest and care in a small girl, guided me gently through the difficult parts of growing up.

Occasionally, from my perch high above the ground, I surveyed the backyards and activities of our neighbors: Mr. and Mrs. Freese, the McCarthys, the Malmgrens, the Hansmanns, and Mrs. Johnson who was teaching me to knit. Half a block away my favorite family, the Lauters, always had time to welcome me into their house or invite me to join Mr. Lauters on their front porch swing. Across Walts

Avenue I could see Phyllis Kreuger's house. Although she was several years older, she always had time to jump rope, play paper dolls, jacks, or "Annie, Annie-I-Over!" Phyllis was my very first "crush."

I haven't changed a lot in the past sixty years. I still need solitude in my life, but, just as I did when I was five, eight, or ten, I also need playmates, kindred spirits, companions, and community. During my parenting years, sometimes the only way to find quiet in a household of eleven people was to lock myself in the bathroom. But that sufficed.

Now I live alone, calling on friends and family for companionship and frequently visiting Blue Cloud Abbey, where friendship, silence, solitude, and prayer help sort out my goals and direction and give a significant focus to my life.

There are times when I am lonely, when I wish I had more companionship. Yet as I get older I realize that need is filled, not from others, but from inside myself. Contentment with the person I have become and trust in the God within who will guide me today and in the future fill up that empty space called loneliness. Tranquility and peace seep into the corners of my existence.

I agree with Henri Nouwen. Solitude is the place where the emergence of the new man and the new woman occurs. But solitude is also the place where an emerging girl and young boy search for answers to the basic questions of life: *Who am I?*

Where am I going? How do I get there? Who is this God who cares about me? It is extremely important for parents and grandparents to guide (and sometimes insist) that young people have time and space to find their own way. We need space, silence, and solitude no matter what our age. The answers that we find as a young child, an adolescent, or a young married person will not necessarily be the same as we move into our sixties, seventies, or eighties. Yet each period of quiet offers an occasion to look deeper into ourselves, finding the God within who will show us the way.

$\mathcal{G}$rowing Old With Friends

Friendship is a full-time occupation.

MALCOLM BOYD

Who are our friends? Are all our friends older, or do we have some young and middle-aged friends also? Is it easier for us to talk to someone our own age? Do we have trouble communicating with children or teens? If that is the case, how much we are missing! Letty Cottin Pogibin says "we need old friends to help us grow old and new friends to help us stay young."

St. Benedict says that all the brothers should be called together for counsel because "the Lord often reveals what is better to the younger." Later in his Rule he reminds us that Samuel and Daniel were mere boys when they gave wise advice to their elders. Benedict knew human nature only too well. It gives a sense of false comfort to be around only those of our own age. They understand us and we understand them. We don't have to explain why or how we do something; we don't have to stretch our imaginations and learn about a new process or way of looking at life. It is as if we are dipped and wrung out in a heavy starch solution and remain stiff and rigid the rest of our life.

I have visited in many complexes where everyone had to be over fifty-five years of age in order to rent or own an apartment or home. True, it was quiet: no screaming voices of children at play, no screeching brakes as teenage drivers arrive or depart from their homes. The occupants feel safer with supposedly no problems due to drugs and alcohol, although people over fifty-five seem to have trouble with those as readily as younger ones.

If all our friends think exactly as we do about world problems, if no one ever challenges us to think of a new way to look at the myriad of questions that arise as the world develops, we will cease to learn and grow. We will not just stagnate; we will slowly slide backward, remaining inflexible and, as our age group dies, find we have fewer and fewer friends.

Younger friends show us new ways of looking at problems, helping us decide how to handle questions or dilemmas that never existed when we were children. It boggles my mind when I think of how future generations will have to handle cloning, euthanasia, or even some new discovery, like mixing the genes of two different species. The night before I wrote this, television news showed a half-sheep, half-goat that had been produced by mixing of the genes.

How will our children and grandchildren's generation handle such ethical problems?

I know my mother, as a child, never dreamed about human beings walking on the moon, living in space, or the atomic bomb, yet in her lifetime those became realities. If she hadn't listened, read, studied, and put all this in context to her values, she would have not only been miserable, but also would have ceased to grow. Like her, I have to listen, read, and study what younger people are saying, not necessarily to approve, but in order to sort out my own value system in relation to science's new discoveries. In order to retain any hope for the world of my children and grandchildren, I have to keep learning.

Living in an artificial world of older people is not conducive to understanding and wisdom. Our world needs wise people. We can't be wise in all areas, but we have an obligation to teach the next generation how to balance and evaluate when problems which we never imagined come into their lives.

Friends are those we use as sounding boards, those who will be honest enough to confront us when we are wrong. Friends, old and young, are the pillars which uphold our base values, encourage and support us when the going gets rough.

> Hand grasps at hand, eye lights eye in good
>   friendship,
> And great hearts expand
> And grow in the sense of this world's life.

RALPH WALDO EMERSON

Gossip or Friendship?

*A loyal friend is a powerful defense;
whoever finds one has indeed found
a treasure.*

SIRACH 6:14

Just recently I read Isabel Huggin's book, *The Elizabeth Stories,* where the child, Elizabeth, overhearing her mother's telephone conversations with her best friend, June, felt violated by her mother's confidences to someone outside the family. No privacy, no protection—just telling all of her bad qualities to the world outside the family.

I smiled when I read the next paragraph:

"Now, of course, I can see how useful those telephone conversations were, and how much more I would have suffered without them. Women like Mavis, married to men like Frank, with children like me . . . women like that needed each other. . . ."

I, too, had a friend like June, a neighbor who had a large family as I did. We discussed our children and their actions and our reactions over the telephone, using each other as sounding boards. Ginny and I learned how to raise our children by listening to each other's experiences. We had no other training, no preparation from our mothers for this stupendous job of raising children, no parenting classes in school, not even today's child psychology articles in magazines or programs on television. Dr. Spock was our only resource, and we lived by his words.

Since her children were several years older than mine, I looked on Ginny as a mentor, someone who could assure me that her children had done those "horrible" things too and the family had lived through it. We were close to the same age, belonged to the same Catholic faith, and shared a similar value system. Many of my child-rearing skills came through our "telephone talks."

As I look back on our friendship, I recognize a 1960s support group, although I never heard that phrase until many years later. Ginny and I gave each other the comfort, communication, understanding, and release which helped us acknowledge that our common sense would see us through.

Now that I am older, I still need those kind of friendships. Sometimes our childhood and young adult friends remain with us; more often we find new ones who give advice, agree, and sometimes disagree with us. Now we don't talk about how to raise our children, we exchange information on aging, sharing our experiences with each other. Above all, our friends share a smile and laugh with us, understanding who we are deep down inside. Friends show us a little portion of God's love.

Go-between

"At the door of the monastery, place a sensible old man who knows how to take a message and deliver a reply, and whose age keeps him from roaming about."

RULE OF BENEDICT CHAP. 66:1,
THE PORTER OF THE MONASTERY

Do you suppose I would qualify as a "sensible old man?" I'm not so sure about age keeping me from roaming about, however. Even though it takes more planning, a longer preparation time, and a good, long rest when I get home, I do roam about the country, learning all kinds of new things and bringing home new ideas.

The trick is to absorb those ideas without using them as a new set of Ten Commandments for Raising Children. Even though I did my share of laying down the law when my own children were little, one of the cardinal rules for grandparents is to let a new generation raise their children for today's world without a constant barrage of advice: "We used to do it this way. . . . when I was young. . . . I would never let my kids do that!"

On the other hand, we have accumulated some wisdom over the years. How do we balance what we know is right and still let the parents make choices based on the values and ethics we have taught them?

Benedict's rules have so much practical advice for parents even after their children have left home. He recommends the porter, the intermediary between the enclosed monastery and the secular world, be an older, judicious, and prudent man who will not be tempted by encountering the visitors who bring the outside world to the cloister. Benedict serves as a spiritual guide with rules and recommendations for us as we age, while the next generation makes their own decisions, forms their own families, and lives their own lives. We do not stop being parents; we just change our *modus operandi.*

I think Benedict is telling me that as one who has lived many years, I should act as the gatekeeper, bringing Christian spirituality into my life as a guide for those who are now in the throes of raising their own family. Can I be a go-between, showing Christ's values by a welcoming example? I am pleased to be a part of my children's lives, even though the problems they encounter differ radically from those I faced as they grew up.

With my new computer which brings e-mail and the internet into my home, can I be trusted to take a message and deliver a reply without interjecting my own advice and rules? I'm trying.

Rich Soil

"A farmer went out sowing. . . . Some of
what he sowed landed on the footpath,
where the birds came along and ate it. . . .
Some seed, finally, landed on good soil
and yielded grain that sprang up to
produce at a rate of thirty- and
sixty- and a hundredfold."

MARK 4:3B-4, 8

It is so easy to let people, events, advertising, the
media, and even well-meaning friends act as the
birds in this parable, not allowing the seed to sprout

and grow in my soul. As I try to balance my day between work, home, and children, the birds gobble up the word and I wonder why I am so tired and stressed out. It isn't so much "keeping up with the Joneses" as it is plowing ahead without taking time to rest and recreate.

Perhaps I need to take a good look at the word *recreation*. There are two kinds: common and personal. Common recreation has to be in conjunction with others; personal is withdrawing from others in order to find silence and solitude, time to listen to God. I may have focused so intently on studying, working, entertaining, and finishing the never-ending daily chores that I have almost become compulsive about my daily work. Jesus saw the need for both kinds of recreation. Many times he left the company of his apostles and the demands of the people to pray and sit with his Father. He also enjoyed a good party, attending the wedding at Cana where celebrations often went on for days.

Real recreation—both common and personal— is a re-creation of ourselves. We have strayed from the path that leaves us relaxed and peaceful and need to tear ourselves away from this drive to *do*. We just need to *be* with others and with God.

Our country's most common form of "recreation" is television, but TV is not a substitute for either common or personal re-creation. In watching TV shows, we withdraw into our own little world, living vicariously with the characters on the screen. These keep our minds busy, leaving no space for us to live within ourselves and giving God a chance to direct us. At best, it can teach us something about our relationships, but if we never use what we have learned, it is a form of standing on a level plain, refusing to move either forward or backward. Eventually, instead of climbing the mountain of our life, we will slide back down the hill.

When my life seems bland, boring, and stagnant (or the opposite: frantic, rushed, and overcommitted) I usually spend three or four days at Blue Cloud Abbey. Leaving all my lists of "to-dos" at home, I take books to read, notepads, pens to write in my journal, and a happy smile as I head north to make sure God's word is falling into good soil.

You don't have to be an oblate or visit a monastery to straighten out your life. You can shut off the phone, letting the answering machine take your calls, and spend some time with your journal. Even a few hours can work wonders. You can be sure that the good soil deep within you will receive the gentle, spring rains of God's grace, allowing the seed to germinate, bringing a harvest of thirty, sixty, or a hundredfold.

Mary and Martha

But the Lord answered, "Martha, Martha . . .
you worry and fret about so many things,
and yet few are needed, indeed only one.
It is Mary who has chosen the better part,
and it is not to be taken away from her."

LUKE 10:41-42

I listened to the priest reading this story last Sunday
and the thought ran through my head: *Martha was the
oldest in the family.* Of course! I was the oldest and I
knew all about oldest daughters being *responsible!*

Mary was obviously the second child and she would naturally overlook what *should* be done in the house and focus on what she wanted to do! Or maybe she was the baby and was spoiled rotten!

Whoa, Cathy! You're running wild and way off the track. I am aware there are a lot of Marthas in the world, including me, who focus on hospitality—food, drink, and comfort—for those who come to visit and we go overboard expecting everyone else to do the same. Am I zeroing in on the work and judging everyone else with my criteria?

There's that old bug-a-boo, *judge,* again. Have I forgotten that Jesus said: "Do not judge, and you will not be judged"? Somewhere in the middle of all this is the half-way point where I can balance my work with prayer while sitting at Jesus' feet.

As a child I was one responsible kid, doing everything I could to be the "good little girl" and make everyone else comfortable. But I am a long way from childhood and I need to look at what is right for me now. Jesus tells us to do some of both—work and pray—and St. Benedict reinforces this teaching with his Holy Rule.

Mary had learned that at first you listened, prayed, dialogued with God, and the rest would naturally follow. She was able to focus on what really needed to be done when Jesus came to visit. She *did* have the "better part."

Yet, as I continued to meditate on this passage of scripture, I realized my cooking, cleaning, and preparing for guests can also be prayer. Everything I do can be a "dialogue with God" if I have that intention as I work—not stirring up my anger because no one is helping. Both avenues are open for me.

This story has several good lessons for me:
Don't expect everyone to view life as I do.
Do the important thing first, listen to Jesus.
Then act upon what I have heard.

If I spend time in prayer before I begin my work, offering my day with its joys, sorrows, work, and play to the God who wants to be an integral part of my life, I am working on my relationship with both God and others.

$\mathcal{A}$ Laughing, Loving Jesus

*"Trust me when I tell you that
whoever does not accept the
kingdom of God as a child will
not enter into it."*

LUKE 18:17

A friend gave me a picture of Jesus and I immediately hung it where I would see it often—a sketch with his hair awry, trimmed beard, a hood flung sideways on his shoulder and the biggest smile I have ever seen.

With laugh lines around his eyes and mouth, this Jesus was having fun. Was he at the wedding at Cana? Was he enjoying some time-out with his disciples? Was he laughing at a joke? I don't know. But you could tell this Jesus had not forgotten how to have fun. He was enjoying himself.

As a little girl I knew how to play games with the neighbor kids, how to have a tea party with my dolls and an imaginary friend, and how to draw pictures, experimenting with chalk on the sidewalk and crayons on plain white paper. Where did all that spontaneity go?

I've tried to look at the child Jesus and wonder how he spent time with his playmates, digging in the dirt or sand, throwing a stick for his dog to fetch, or just playing ball with the neighborhood gang. This artist's rendering of a grown-up thirty-year-old Jesus had kept the joy and verve of childhood and I wanted part of that gift.

Somewhere over the years, life got too serious and I forgot how to play—at least play without feeling guilty. Perhaps the German/English ancestry poked its nose into my psyche. Home and society did a good job of teaching me to take care of everybody else first and only use what's left for myself. During the hectic years of raising a family I found very little "time left over."

Becoming a Benedictine oblate, reading and meditating on Benedict's Rule, helped me throw off this mantle of guilt. It allowed me to see the joy that can come from balancing work, study, pray, and play. Several times a year I visit a Benedictine monastery. I go for the solitude, silence, and prayerful atmosphere, but also for the camaraderie, the humor, the joy of life that I find in the monks. Their life is one of prayer, work, and study, yet they have taught me much about having a day off, the agape love of a family, the joy and healing power of a good laugh. Norman Cousins, in his book *Anatomy of an Illness*, started the research into the healing qualities of laughter. Today we can find many books on that subject. Laughter and humor balance the sorrow and grief in our lives.

Even today I get so caught up in "necessary" activities that I often need a reminder to relax and recreate. It takes training to think in terms of fun and toys. Once a week I say: "Have you done anything to play this week, Cathy?" It could be a trip to the art center, walking near the river, or leaving the supper dishes in the sink and sitting down to watch *M.A.S.H.*; it could be a class on surfing the internet or renting a Bob Hope or Danny Thomas movie.

My family seems to realize my need for remembering my childhood fun. A daughter gave me a fabric-covered box with five or six fun toys including a statue of two clowns doing a balancing act, Loony Tunes paper clips, a Tweetie Bird rubber ball, and the *pièce de résistance*—a Bugs Bunny curly, plastic straw. I immediately used the straw to drink a root beer float, my favorite teenage drink. She encouraged me to add some more things that have no earthly use except to bring a smile to my lips. Every time I look at the box, my spirits lift.

Spending money for toys is especially hard. Growing up in the Great Depression still throws that mantle of guilt on my back, but I am learning. Perhaps by the time I am done with this book I will be able to report a few more playthings for my toy box.

Whatever it is, there is more fun—and as a consequence, more joy and peace—in my life. I'm not in charge of everyone and everything; having fun and playing is as necessary for a full life as work, study, and prayer. Heaven will be a mixture of all these, and more.

$\mathcal{V}$iolence and Our Grandchildren

*Learn to do good, search for justice,
discipline the violent, be just to the
orphan, plead for the widow.*

ISAIAH 1:17

These words from Isaiah make me wonder: What was discipline in the time of Isaiah? How do I define discipline today? What is discipline? Is spanking wrong? How about a pat on the behind? What deterrents to a child's unsuitable behavior can we use rather than physically hitting them? Are there ways of showing a child how to act that teaches them more effectively than physical violence?

If you are like me you must wonder sometimes how all the violence our grandchildren are exposed to will affect their lives. Television and movies come to mind first of all because entertainment—music, videos, and movies—seems to be such a vital part of their days. Depending on where we live, violence in the streets due to gangs and drugs have escalated our fears.

As much as we want to deny it, violence between mother and father, parents and children has begun to come out of the closet. Spousal and parental abuse are no longer topics to be hidden, but require reporting to the appropriate authorities. How can we be part of the solution and not part of the problem?

This is such a new field for grandparents we are likely to revert to saying: *The way we raised our kids was good enough. Why can't they do the same as we did?* I haven't got answers to all of these questions, but I do believe we have a very real obligation to search for them. As our knowledge of psychology increases, we have a duty to study and use it to help not only the world, but our immediate families. We need to find a measure of peace in our relationships.

Violence breeds violence. If I spank or hit to get a lesson across, then the child has learned to do the same. It is one of those generational lessons that go on and on, helping no one and often breeding an unending cycle of violence for decades after I am gone.

I am aware that changing the way I have always disciplined the children in my care is a big undertaking.

I had thought my days of child raising were over when my own children left home, thinking it was up to the next generation to raise their own. Now that I have time to sit back and evaluate the methods I used thirty or forty years ago, I know there are better ways to react.

Certainly there has to be discipline. Grandma and Grandpa have household rules that need to be reinforced more than once when young grandchildren visit. Yelling, screaming, and hitting only promotes fear in a child and does nothing to form a loving, healthy relationship between grandparent and grandchild. A calm "No," or "We don't do that in our house," will suffice. With a calm response we are teaching the child that a disapproved action can be stopped without verbal or physical violence. At the same time we are growing in our own wisdom, learning to "discipline the violent" in new, more effective ways.

It is certainly O.K. for us, as grandparents, to censor the television programs and the web sites our grandchildren view in our home; in fact, it is a definite obligation. There will be plenty of choices for the child as he grows more independent, but basic values will still be part of those choices.

Grandparents are a long way from being done with raising children. We can make a choice: either we sit back and grouch about how the next generation is raising their children, or we can learn how to use the work of many psychologists to help the world get better and better, even if in incremental steps. What will we choose?

Prayer and Art

*There is nothing so secular it
cannot be sacred.*

MADELEINE L'ENGLE

Perhaps you are someone who cannot see any
connection between prayer and art. Yet there is
absolutely nothing in the world that does not or
cannot have a place in prayer.

We all know that the purpose of statues, stations of the cross, madonnas, icons, and stained glass windows is to turn our thoughts to God. In ancient times these were used to teach the stories of our faith to illiterate people. Even today they are symbols that speak to our unconscious, no matter how much learning we have acquired along the way.

Music, too, is an art that is a basic component of our worship. It needs to be experienced at a level deeper than our conscious minds. The songs chosen for a certain liturgy have the power either to bring us into community or to turn us off and let our minds wander. When I was going to a Catholic school, the sisters always told us that the person who sang (at that time it was the choir) prayed twice. God likes to hear our voices raised in song! Now that we are all encouraged to sing, we can all receive the benefit of those twice-told prayers even if we aren't melodic enough to be in the choir. God loves me even if I can't carry a tune.

Listening to music can also be a form of prayer—of course, it depends on the type of music. If I let myself go, empty myself of preconceived notions, and allow myself to truly feel what the music is saying, classical music can also be a form of prayer for me.

Madeleine L'Engle, who writes for both children and adults, says a Christian artist sees art—be it writing, composing, sculpting, painting, or photography—as being for the glory of God. How many of us can say that we see our daily work as being for the glory of God, even though we say we are Christians? It's something to think about.

Music, art, and the beauty of nature can all be starting points for prayer. My crystal collection—beautifully formed calcite, quartz, tourmaline, and pyrite—is a case in point. Several of these crystals sit in my prayer corner where a light from the candle plays upon their faceted beauty, reminding me that God has a plan for me, just as he has a plan for those sparkling gems.

Many years ago my daughter studied in France and I spent two weeks sightseeing with her as my guide. At one of the museums, Colleen insisted that we stop and see Monet's paintings. I had never really seen original masterpieces before, so I was unprepared for the emotional effect that comes from paintings of such magnitude. "Water Lilies" was displayed in two large circular rooms completely covered with Monet's impressions of his garden water-lily pond and the play of light on it. Done over his lifetime, the shades of blue and green, with recurring yellows, reds, and blacks, showed his life progression, his turning points, his changing style, his temperament, his depressions and failures. At the same time I could see my life progression, my turning points, depressions, and failures as my style and temperament changed. I felt like I was almost part of the painting. It was an experience of God's action in my life, a revelation of God's love for me—a truly religious experience. It was a prayer.

Shakers, a religious community in New England, believe the work of the hands has to reflect a moral order, and that the outward appearance of things reveals the inner spirit. Since Shakers lead a communal, celibate life, there are only a few older ladies left, yet people are attracted not only to their teachings and handiwork, but also to the way they live.

Simplicity is a Shaker hallmark. A spiritual foundation based on their sense of thrift, order, cleanliness, invention, and self-sufficiency has taught them to make their heavenly ideals a working part of their everyday life and work. This is evident in all their furniture. "Whenever they put their hands to work, they also put their hearts to God," says June Sprigg, curator of Shaker exhibition at N.Y. Whitney Museum of American Art. This too is prayer.

Maybe this is a new way of thinking about art for you as it was to me. But just seeing the beauty in what someone else has made has been an opening to a whole new way of praying for me. Perhaps it can be for you as well.

✐ood and Lovely

A woman brought in a vase of perfumed
oil and stood behind him at his feet,
weeping so that her tears fell upon his
feet. Then she wiped them with her hair,
kissing them and perfuming them with
her oil.

LUKE 7:37B-38

The unnamed woman's action of pouring a pound of
perfume on Jesus' feet and wiping it with her hair
sometimes seems such a waste of money to us.
Wasn't it, as Judas complained, almost an ignoring of
the poor who lived all around them and followed
Jesus with such hope? Wouldn't it have been better to
sell the perfume and feed the hungry?

In Jimmy Carter's *Living Faith*, he reflects on this
passage. He says this incident showed him that the

woman's great love for Jesus prompted her action. He pointed out there are times we need to break out of the practical and predictable ways we live and show those we love how much they mean to us. The Bible describes this kind of love as *kalos*, "good and lovely." We need to delight our loved ones with "good and lovely" surprises, showing our deeper feelings through creative actions. Pouring perfume worth a year's wages was an action so out of the ordinary that even two thousand years later we intuitively know the depth of her love.

I was suddenly aware that the practical, left-brain-focused Cathleen very seldom thought of unpredictable, wild, and far-out ideas—let alone carried them out. I can be challenged and rise to the occasion, but I tend to go in straight-line, predictable ways.

Carter questioned: "Within my own talent and realm of possibilities, what can I find to do that would be good and lovely?" Reflecting on his question has helped me to be more spontaneous with my family and to grow in confidence to use the gift of writing that God has given me.

My sudden idea to rent a lakeside cabin and invite my children and their families to join me for a few days was an answer. It gave the whole family a goal which put a breath of sorely-needed relaxation into their busy summers. I don't have the energy to babysit, clean, or cook as I did when I was younger, so I can't do that any more for my children and grandchildren. Yet nourishing our relationships can take other, less active forms. The joy of being together for a few days provided us with the necessary hours in which all generations could become friends, not just parent/grandparent/child. Now I have many hours of memories to draw on, memories which will contribute a depth to our love when we talk on the phone or exchange e-mail notes, sustaining us even though we are half a continent apart.

I am also learning not to let my left brain (the thinking side) block my response to God's call to me to create "the good and the lovely." Madeline L'Engle tells her creative writing classes: "Don't think. Just write." Here's how I try to put her words into practice. As I prepare for my daily writing, I put my hands in my lap, shut my eyes, and let go of all my questions, worries, and schedules. I spend a few minutes meditating, not thinking of anything, allowing myself to empty my cup so that God can fill it. I pray, "Lord, put your words into my fingers. Let me be a channel of your Word."

Then it is off to writing. Some things will stay; some will go, but the words that need to be put into print will remain. The finished product will be a collaboration, a co-creation. God and I together have produced something new.

To find new ways to handle problems or find new solutions does not require "thinking" skills. I was being called to change. What does this have to do with growing old? Well, it is never too late to change. To be my own self, following his plan for my life is all that God asks of me. The result will indeed be good and lovely.

Heritage

Know thyself.

ANONYMOUS

Although the inscription above has been attributed to Plato and was carved on the temple of Apollo at Delphi, we aren't sure just who wrote it. Nevertheless the truth, "Know thyself," is the basis of coming to terms with where we are going. Without self-knowledge, how can we grasp the fact that we were made not only to live, but also to die?

Working on my family genealogy and the stories that accompany the lives of my ancestors, I have come to know myself better and recognize this search as a prayer leading me closer to God. Delving into my heritage reveals not only the life stories of my parents and ancestors, but also provides clues to my inner being where God resides.

This genealogy work prompts me to ask, "Why am I here? Where am I going? Who has been an important part of my journey?" Such questions are part of a deep search for meaning, a search for the God who made me. As I near the end of my life, this search becomes more insistent.

Some of my questions are answered as I look at my heritage. A couple of summers ago my daughter and I took a trip to Ireland hoping to find out more about the Irish side of our ancestry. Since our return home I have pondered the feeling that my predominant genes must be Irish. The deep feeling I experienced as I stood on the land of my great-grandmother, a five-mile-long island off the coast of Ireland, convinced me the Irish had contributed much to my search for meaning. My Irish heritage emphasized the importance of education, stories, symbols, and parables. It gave me a willingness to risk and a firm belief in the love and steadfastness of God.

Yet my mother, a full-blooded German, gave me determination, fortitude, and the same deep belief that education should be a top priority in my life. Both sides of the family instilled a firm belief that in the Catholic Church I would find God. But at the same time they also taught me by their acceptance of other beliefs that each individual finds truth in his own way. Another's path may not be the same as mine, but at the end of our lives we all get a glimpse of truth. Ultimately I am a blending of these two cultures, two sets of genes; an individual who listened, absorbed, and formed my unique personality to be the person I am today.

What did your parents teach you? What did you learn, almost by osmosis, from the culture around you? Sometimes it is hard to tell the difference. Drawing from a variety of sources, we pick and choose, sometimes subconsciously, taking what we need for our growth and development. Our work as we get older is to discard those outgrown rituals and rules and take on what pertains to our adulthood, what will lead us to truth.

Coming Into the Light

*"Whoever does the truth
comes out into the light,
so that what he is doing
may plainly appear as done in God."*

JOHN 3:21

Visiting a monastery a couple of years ago I was eating with a group of monks when one asked me: "Have you anyone special in your life now that your husband has been gone twenty years?" Without hesitation I replied: "Not so you could notice!"

The rest of the monks laughed and said: "Good for you, Cathy. You should have told him it was none of his business." That really didn't occur to me, however, because those men are good friends, and I knew it was said in a spirit of love and interest in my life, as well as just plain curiosity.

I did go on to say: "I believe in answering questions when they are asked as truthfully as I can." It's a belief I have come to treasure the more I reflect on how carefully it was avoided in my family of origin. So much of my childhood was lived under the unwritten rule: "We don't talk about that!" None of the relatives would tell me their ages, including my mother and father. I was a married woman before I knew that family friends had a "Mongoloid" child. I was well into my fifties with an alcoholic sister before I knew my grandfather and uncle were alcoholics.

Growing up in an atmosphere of repression where telling the truth is avoided—be it alcoholism, hereditary diseases, or one's age—produces emotionally undernourished adults. Unable to form mutually-nurturing relationships with loved ones, they raise their children in the same pattern of half-truths. It is time for these false fronts to be abandoned.

At the same monastery one of the monks commented, "This place is full of secrets." I would challenge that monastic community, just as I would challenge all families, to break the cycle of secrets, to take the risk and tell the truth. If we claim to be Christians, then we should follow Christ's example. Truth was an integral part of his relationships with others.

It is not easy to bring up family secrets with our siblings or parents, but, at the appropriate time, a clearing of the air can bring families closer together. You may ask, "What is the appropriate time?" Patience in letting God handle the timing, combined with prayer to discern his plan, will eventually answer that question. Sometimes the suitable opportunity never comes; that is God's answer. If it is to happen, the opening will come.

Sound judgments in future generations depend on our actions today. Our integrity depends on whether we are seen as credible by the younger generation, even as we take care that our answers are appropriate for the age of the child. Being open and honest with our grandchildren will do more to teach them how to be open and honest than all our lectures. Even as children and adolescents see television programs and movies which are diametrically opposed to our values, they still have absorbed what we are trying to teach. We can do no more than show what we believe; from there on it is their decision. If we live by the truth, we will show light to our descendants. As John said, "The man who lives by the truth comes out into the light."

Pride

*Then the devil led (Jesus) to Jerusalem,
set him on the parapet of the Temple, and
said to him, "If you are the Son of God,
throw yourself down from here, for
Scripture has it, 'He will bid his angels
watch over you;' and again, 'With their
hands they will support you, that you
may never stumble on a stone.'"*

LUKE 4:9-11

I had heard the gospel for the First Sunday of Lent so often that the words didn't penetrate my upset about being late for Mass. I had come to church in plenty of time, and about five minutes before the service was to begin I suddenly remembered I had promised to pick up a lady and bring her too. My gasp startled the people around me as much as it did me. I grabbed my purse and ran for the door, telling the priest to call her and say I was on my way.

We were only about five minutes late, but my concentration was shot. How could I forget her? There were all kinds of excuses, but the homily put it all in perspective.

The devil tempted Jesus three times: the first time with food, since Jesus, after forty days fasting, was pretty hungry. The second time he tried to seduce him with power. Again his wiles were futile. But the third time, it was pride, a sin that sneaks in when we are most vulnerable. The devil, knowing Jesus was human as well as divine, tried to get him to tempt his Father: "You are so good that your Father will protect you from all the usual results that afflict the rest of humankind."

I felt my face grow hot, and then an inner smile of recognition blossomed. Thank heavens there was grace enough for me to realize that pride had reared its ugly head as I had waited calmly and patiently for the eucharist to begin without thinking of anyone else. I had been so busy creating my own scenario of a "good Christian" that I had ignored anyone outside of my immediate orbit. I was my own god, which was exactly what the devil had wanted to create. With no concern for the rest of the world, self-praise could sneak in and steer me away from the humility that is so necessary to enter the kingdom of heaven.

Sometimes God teaches me a lesson in surprising ways.

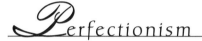erfectionism

From all your idols I will cleanse you.

EZEKIEL 36:25B

From what idols does God have to cleanse me?

Probably the idol of myself. I have been self-reliant all through my life. From the time I was two years old and informed my aunt who was trying to dress me, "By self, Aunt La La, by self!" to the years after Jim's death where I thought I had to raise our nine children by myself.

Gradually I learned that without God, I was helpless. God showed me through relatives, in-laws, friends, and especially the church that thinking I could do it "by self!" was indeed an idol. Hillary Clinton had it right: "It takes a village to raise a child."

For me to believe that I could be perfect, be both a mother *and* a father to our four girls and five boys, was to believe that I was as good as God. Even to write that makes me smile. It can't be. Only God is perfect and he doesn't expect us to be anything except what he created us to be—human beings. Just like Jesus on his way to Golgotha, we fall, take a deep breath, and pull ourselves up to try again. God's unconditional, healing love is there for me to accept or reject.

Which do I choose today?

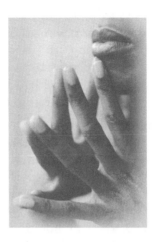

Judgment

Every one of you who judges another is inexcusable. By your judgment you convict yourself, since you do the very same things.

ROMANS 2:1

What a list this scripture verse brought up! I always have plenty of opinions on what the other guy should do, berating them for "doing the wrong thing." There is the city council who seems to have their priorities all mixed up, the grandchild who in her search for independence stretched it too far, or the sibling who is reacting to our mother's death in a far different way than I am. Someone's "early" pregnancy, abortion, "shacking up" with a boyfriend, divorce, second and third marriages—the slate goes on and on. If I go this far, then I had better look into myself—and here is where I run into trouble.

There is a great JUDGE inside me, who keeps a running tally of all my stupid mistakes and my sins of omission as well as commission. At the top of the list are the times I have not been "perfect." That same judge holds court with siblings, friends, relatives, and well-known figures as defendants, blaming others for their mistakes and sins while finding excuses for mine. By blaming others I take the focus away from myself and no one will know how terrible I am.

I have to keep reminding myself that I am not God. He made me a human being and asked that I keep working *toward* perfection, even though I will not *be* perfect until I am in heaven.

After all these years psychologists are agreeing with Paul. They call it *projection* when we take our own shadow side and berate those around us for the failings that are our own. If I am truly honest I look deeply only into myself, see my own sins and ask God for his forgiveness. I have no right to judge others. Each person's life experiences influences their actions. Only God knows what is in the heart.

Remind me, Lord, that I am not you. You made me a human being and asked that I keep working toward perfection, even though I will not get all the way until I am in heaven. My only job is to accept and love. The letter to the Romans has it right: *"It is yourself that you condemn when you judge others. . . . "*

Perhaps my word for today should read *"when you love others, you love yourself, even with all your failings."*

Condemnation
and Forgiveness

Once more have pity on us,
tread down our faults;
throw all our sins
to the bottom of the sea.

MICAH 7:19

As I listened to President Clinton admitting on national television he had an affair with a young girl, that he had lied to not only his wife but to the

American people, I waited for those two fateful words that never came: "I'm sorry." That event led me to consider the many aspects of judgment, condemnation, and forgiveness.

Seventy years has helped me realize that my first reaction is usually one I picked up early in life—judgment. But I've learned that words and judgments arising from feelings of shock or disappointment are usually not the result of due reflection. Over the first few days, as I pondered the difference between right and wrong, I concluded that I disliked the way Clinton excused himself: "Legally, I did nothing wrong." I was not looking for the legal aspect of this case. I waited for the "I'm sorry," the "Please forgive me."

I wanted to let it go, but having raised nine children, I knew that when one of them crossed the line I couldn't ignore it. Some discipline had to be administered. That is true for all of us, no matter what our age. No one, not even the President of the United States, is above the moral law.

It is not possible to be perfect. We try and sometimes we succeed, but because we are human, sometimes we fail. After each failure we pick ourselves up and try again. Somehow we have forgotten the obligation to make amends: to admit our sin, express our sorrow, and vow to improve. On the other side of the ledger, I can understand addictions and compulsions that are seemingly impossible to change without the guidance and help of support groups, counselors, and most of all, God.

That August night when the president went on television to speak to the American people, I wondered if very many listeners were stepping back from their immediate reaction and reflecting on how Jesus might have acted. When the woman caught in adultery was brought to him, he did not lash out at her, quoting Moses' edict that she was to be stoned to death. As the Son of God, he could have been judgmental, just as the "talking heads" were doing to Clinton. He chose to ignore the crowd, saying nothing, and bent down to write in the sand at his feet. You could almost cut the silence with a knife.

Perhaps Jesus meant to calm the mob who had gathered around her. Perhaps he was writing down the sins of her accusers. We don't know; the Bible does not tell us. But we do know what action he took. After a long period of silence he finally spoke: "Let the man among you who has no sin be the first to cast a stone at her." Then he bent over and began writing again.

The men, beginning with the elders who had brought her, began to drift away, until only Jesus was left. Straightening up, he asked her:

"Woman, where did they all disappear to? Has no one condemned you?"

"No one, sir," she answered.

Jesus said, "Nor do I condemn you. You may go. But from now on, avoid this sin" (Jn 8:10b-11).

He was able to "throw all her sins in the bottom of the sea." Jesus, the Son of God, loved her unconditionally, forgiving her, only telling her to sin no more. She could choose to follow his advice, but because of God's gift of free will, the decision was up to her. Surely, if I want to be a follower of Christ, I must do the same, even as I pray each day that the president will find the strength to follow Jesus' advice, "sin no more."

No, this story does not answer all the qualms people had about the adulterous woman, any more than it answers the qualms I felt about Clinton that night. Only time and prayer will show me how to let go of this judgmental tendency and allow forgiveness to come into my heart. I'm never done learning.

Forgiving Myself

Then Peter came up and asked him, "Lord, when my brother wrongs me, how often must I forgive him? Seven times?" "No," Jesus replied, "not seven times; I say, seventy times seven times."

MATTHEW 18:21-22

Ordinarily our parish celebrates daily eucharist each morning, but today, because our priest was on vacation, we celebrated a communion service with a lay person presiding. I really didn't want to get up and venture out, but, as usual when I procrastinate, my conscience pushed me out of bed and I was there. (At least my body was there.) Only about six people came, but as we went through the liturgy of the word my mind was far from the service I was attending.

I was blue and depressed, wondering how I had ever gotten into so many projects that I really had no time for myself. It definitely was one of my down days. Feeling sorry for myself was the top priority of the morning. Blame was flying all around. I blamed my parents for teaching me to say yes to everyone who had a request, the people who asked me to be on these committees, and the fast-paced world around me. Even though I promised myself to say no to the next phone call, I was upset because I had overextended myself.

Somehow I had a feeling that most of the blame should be landing squarely on my back. Whose fault was it if I had taken on more projects than I could manage? Surely my own. Would I ever get it right? Again I had forgotten my priorities and tried to please everyone around me instead of following God's will. My self-worth plummeted. I still expected perfection in myself.

The leader read the gospel of Matthew: "How often must I forgive my brother?" I suddenly woke up. Of course! It wasn't my brother (or my parents, friends, or the world) that I needed to forgive, it was myself! Again I was my own worst enemy, expecting myself to be perfect and piling on the unrealistic guilt.

My first step was to admit I've made mistakes. The second one was to accept my humanity and realize God loves me even if I bite off more than I can chew. If God can forgive my stumbling journey to him, then who am I to refuse to forgive myself? Do I require more of myself than God does? Forgiveness does not always have to be for the other person; forgiving myself is equally important. Jesus' seventy-times-seven applies to me as well as my brothers and sisters.

Each day is a new beginning and I can forgive myself each night, just as God does. If God loves and forgives me (and I truly believe he does) then who am I to refuse God's unconditional love and forgiveness for myself ? All I need to do is to let my human frailties fall into the chasm of his love. His light will stay with me.

Humility

O Lord, my heart is not proud
nor are my eyes haughty;
I busy not myself with great things
nor with things too sublime for me.

PSALM 131:1

Whenever I pray this psalm I have a hard time with this first verse. Even though I would love to be a model of modesty and mildness and, of course, free from arrogance, I have to admit that I am a long way from Mother Teresa. Her devotion to the sick and dying, her calm self-acceptance, and her ability to speak out when the occasion called for it have long been a model for me. As always, however, my actions are often far removed from my goals.

St. Benedict has some good advice for people like me. He quotes Psalm 131 as he begins the seventh chapter of his Rule. His lengthy teaching on humility and succinct instructions are food for many meditations. The twelve steps of humility are a lifetime process, bringing us closer and closer to the God who loves us so much.

Step 1: that a man keeps the fear of God always before his eyes. . . .

Step 2: that a man loves not his own will nor takes pleasure in the satisfaction of his desires. . . .

The first and second steps, according to Benedict, remind us that we must always keep the fear of God before our eyes. Fear does not mean the first definition we find in the dictionary: "a feeling of agitation and anxiety caused by the presence or imminence of danger." On the contrary it relates more to the third definition: "extreme reverence or awe, as toward a supreme power." Benedict wants us to remember that even our secret actions are known, inspiring us not to do our own will, but only the will of our Father in heaven. Even though sometimes it seems as if God is allowing us to wander down the wrong path, eventually there will be an accounting, just as a loving father corrects his child. Appropriate discipline or punishment helps us to let go of our own desires and to imitate Jesus: "I have come not to do my own will, but the will of him who sent me."

Step 3: that a man submits to his superior in all obedience for the love of God. . . .

Step 4: that in this obedience . . . his heart quietly embraces suffering and endures it without weakening or seeking escape. . . .

The third step asks us to submit to our superiors for the love of God. In the fourth step, he shows us this obedience requires an acceptance of suffering. This last is a difficult one for me. Not to run away from the pains and hurts of life, to turn and embrace the suffering as I unite it with Jesus' sufferings, requires a complete turnaround from my ordinary reaction of trying to eliminate grief, anxiety and heartaches.

I believe God is asking us to balance our sufferings: using what we have learned in psychology and science to understand and alleviate our pain, but not expecting complete deliverance. The remainder is the portion we are asked to embrace. The virtue of patience is certainly required during this step.

Step 5: that a man does not conceal from his abbot any sinful thoughts . . . or any wrongs committed in secret. . . .

The fifth step asks us to confess our sins to another. Even though modern society uses a therapist or psychiatrist (or perhaps the "spill-it-all-out" talk shows) as one who will help them through the dark times, as a Catholic I find a great need for the sacrament of reconciliation. To be able to tell a priest of my failures and receive an outpouring of grace to help me change is a necessary step in my healing. I have a feeling this is true for most of us, even though this sacrament has lost favor with many Catholics.

$\mathcal{M}$ore About Humility

"For everyone who exalts himself
will be humbled,
but the one who humbles himself
will be exalted."

LUKE 14:11

Luke considered this statement of Jesus to be so important he elaborated on it in two different chapters of his gospel. St. Benedict also devoted his longest chapter to this topic of *humility*. His steps six through twelve continue to outline a map which brings us closer and closer to God.

> Step 6: that a monk is content with the lowest and most menial treatment and regards himself as a poor and worthless workman in whatever task he is given. . . .

> Step 7: that a man not only admits with his tongue, but is also convinced in his heart that he is inferior to all and of less value. . . .

As I move on in the path of humility, these statements from the Rule of Benedict help me see the games I play with others, using manipulation as a way to get what I want. Often I feel superior to others, find and use their weak spots to run the world my way. An overly ambitious and extremely competitive person is not part of God's agenda. Trina Paulus, in *Hope for the Flowers*, wrote a parable about a caterpillar who climbs over his brothers and sisters on a tree in order to be the first and only one on the top. All the way he keeps kicking those who are right behind, refusing to let others reach the topmost branch. Not until the end of the story does the little insect realize that God had a much better future planned for him. Toward the end of my life I, like the caterpillar, have become aware of my fragile existence, my dependence on God and my peers. I believe that someday I too will turn into a beautiful butterfly.

Step 8: that a monk does only what is endorsed by the common rule of the monastery and the example set by his superiors. . . .

Step eight refers to the penchant we have for bragging, for being "top dog" in a group or community. It is difficult to find a good balance between self-worth and glorifying myself. I want others to know the good things I have done, the time I have spent helping others. Yet Benedict asks that we not draw attention or be a law to ourselves. Using my God-given talents and understanding my own self-worth without boasting requires honesty and prayer. He uses the word *content* to describe someone who is making progress in humility. I need to be content with where I am just at this moment. I am on my way, and that is what God is asking of me.

Step 9: that a monk controls his tongue and remains silent. . . .

Step 10: that he is not given to ready laughter. . . .

Step 11: that a monk speaks gently . . . seriously and with becoming modesty. . . .

Silence, gentle laughter, and humble bearing in steps nine, ten, and eleven give me useful ways to practice humility. Our tongues can be used to hurt someone else, just as laughter which results from pointedly running down another race, the opposite sex, or a different nationality can be one of our worst faults. Silence might mean shutting off the television and radio for a portion of the day. It also might mean shutting off the compulsive talking which gives me no time to hear what God has to say. Benedict asks that we speak gently, briefly, seriously and, above all, with kindness.

> Step 12: that a monk always manifests humility in his bearing no less than in his heart. . . .

What is on the inside of the person shows on the outside. If we are working toward humility by these twelve steps, our behavior and conduct will reflect this. Our goal of humility is a never-ending project. We must never forget to take off our masks, be open and honest not only about our accomplishments but also our mistakes. If we can make this a habit that is so deeply a part of us, we can always count on the love and mercy of God.

These twelve steps of humility are a lifetime project. I can't make the mistake of thinking I can do it all by myself. Only by God's amazing grace, by his constant love and awareness of my helplessness, can I hope to find the God who will turn my blindness into seeing.

> Amazing grace, how sweet the sound
> that saved a wretch like me.
> I once was lost, but now am found,
> was blind, but now I see. . . .
>
> JOHN NEWTON

Faith and Fog

"He spread a thick fog between you and the Egyptians, and made the sea go back on them."

JOSHUA 24:7

When I read this passage I could see and feel the "thick fog" that rose between the Israelites and the Egyptians, the drops of water that they could feel on their forehead as they rushed to get away from their enemies. They were cornered—the only way to go was straight ahead into the Red Sea. They looked with amazement as the wall of water formed on their right and another on their left, leaving a path through which they could flee.

What faith Moses had, to lead them fearlessly through that path, faith that the God of Abraham and Sarah, Isaac and Rachel, Jacob and Leah would save his chosen people from drowning! What faith each one of the Israelites had, to follow this charismatic leader and to trust Yahweh with the lives of each man, woman, and child in the whole train of people.

Would I have had such trust? Do I have faith the size of a mustard seed today to follow what you are asking me to do?

Wisdom

For the age that is honorable comes not
   with the passing of time,
nor can it be measured in terms of years.
Rather, understanding is the hoary crown
   for men,
and an unsullied life, the attainment of
   old age.

WISDOM 4:8-9

At certain stages of life, men and women are supposed to have learned certain things. The trouble is, we don't always absorb those truths according to schedule. Some adults of forty have not outgrown their adolescent ways of thinking; others at forty have moved far beyond those youthful ways and show a wisdom and maturity usually seen in later years.

The writer of the book of Wisdom is very much aware of this human quality; he teaches that common sense, clear thinking, and enlightenment come at different ages for different people. Using Solomon as the mentor for maturing individuals, the writer says grey hairs and an untarnished life is a goal of a ripe old age, but does not come automatically with the passage of years.

Solomon was a young man when he succeeded his father David as king. When the Lord told him in a dream to ask for anything he wanted and promised to give it to him, Solomon—even as he realized his humanity, his penchant for sinfulness—asked for "an understanding heart to judge your people and to distinguish right from wrong."

As I approach old age I too search for wisdom and an understanding heart. Simplicity, acceptance, forgiveness (of ourselves and others), and the realization of my priorities are all part of the aging process. Reminiscing on my past, musing on what I have learned (even though each day brings new insights), brings a fresh way of looking at my life today.

God grant me the serenity
to accept the things I cannot change,
the courage to change the things I can,
and the wisdom to know the difference.

Reinhold Neibuhr's prayer can—and probably should be—our mantra, our prayer as we open ourselves to follow God's will.

𝒫atience

*Hoping for what we cannot see means
awaiting it with patient endurance.*

ROMANS 8:25

Patience—the word carries a lifelong legacy. There
have been so many struggles to be calm in turbulent
times, to find self-control when anger erupts, to be
content when our hoped-for results do not appear,
and to endure inconvenience without complaint.

As a parent, there is always an aspect of hope contained in our patience. As a grandparent, I not only need the hope I had when raising my children, but I often have to put in an extra dash of willingness, too, just to hang in there. Before I can understand the young generation—their inexhaustible energy, their curiosity, and even their ability to embrace the newest novelty that Madison Avenue can project—I actually have to draw back and do some deep thinking. I can be excited with them and for them as they discover new possibilities in their life, but, no matter how much I love them, some of their goals and actions raise a flag of disapproval.

This is where patience comes in. I am not one but two generations removed from my beloved grandchildren. It may be a cliché, but times have changed with exponential leaps, changes which demand that we solve a whole new series of ethical problems.

All this comes as I grow older, more-or-less reluctant to change my ideas about the universe. As my body slows down, I am asked to provide ethical consideration to all kinds of new discoveries and inventions. It seems easier to register disapproval than to understand.

Yet my grandchildren deserve to hear my reflections on life just as I learned from my grandparents, peers, and parents. Fundamental values of life, love, and God remain the same. We—and our grandchildren—have to apply those values to the problems of the twenty-first century.

Basically our grandchildren are like us. God has given them a mind to question the status quo and the ability to build on the values we teach them. If we do not have the patience to portray our analysis of a situation, how can we expect them to make relevant decisions on topics which we were never required to make? After we are gone, how do they make decisions on subjects unknown to us at this time?

Through our ability to talk about the dilemmas we have experienced, the times we made mistakes and had to ask forgiveness from others and the times we had to let go of our tendency to control and rely on only God's grace, we are helping the emerging generation form their own values.

$\mathcal{A}$ New Heart

I shall give you a new heart,
and put a new spirit in you;
I shall remove the heart of stone from
   your bodies
and give you a heart of flesh instead.

EZEKIEL 36:26

My new heart of flesh longs for you, Lord, and aches
for justice and peace among all human beings. But if
all I do is "feel" with this heart you have given me, I

am not following your way. Part of my heart is still that "heart of stone." Believing, feeling sympathy, hurting inside is not enough, is it, Lord? If I am your hands in today's world, then all that empathy and sympathy is worth nothing unless I act—to relieve the pain, hurt, and suffering of others.

St. Paul says: "If I have not charity" everything else is worthless. Charity or love is action—showing by my actions that I have love. Love is more, much more, than a feeling inside me. It is, according to Thomas Aquinas, "willing the good of another." When I love, I do everything possible to help my beloved. How much do I love?

ℐnsomnia

*Lift up your hands to the holy place
and bless the Lord through the night.*

PSALM 134:2

Two o'clock a.m. and I can't sleep. Why not? I lead a fairly quiet life, taking care of myself by eating properly, balancing the day between prayer, study, and work. I exercise to keep my aging body in good health. I enjoy companionship through e-mail and letters to and from my children and friends. I stop to thank God for the blessings of the day. Yet here I am, halfway through the night, wide awake, worrying about the next day or the next week or perhaps even the next year. My mind races at 100 m.p.h. Even though I know writing in my journal can soothe the savage beast that is determined to devour these hours of rest, my body refuses to get out of bed.

I'm too tired to move.

God didn't mean for human beings to work in the middle of the night.

A thought challenges me: *Why do you always have to know why, Cathy? Why can't you just accept this as a time God might want to talk with you?*

Surprisingly this relieves my tension. I do not fight the sleeplessness; I rest in God's arms, just "patiently waiting and tenderly abiding," just as Sr. Macrina Wiederkehr recommends. My breath flows gently, in and out . . . in and out . . . my breath brings the Spirit in and the racing thoughts out . . . in and out . . . in and out, not just to myself, but to the whole world.

The word comes:

"Lift up your hands to the holy place
and bless the Lord through the night."

I bless the Lord through the night and I am at peace—even as my elbow creaks and my body hurts. The pain joins Jesus' sufferings, the world's redemption. Sleep comes in like Carl Sandburg's "Fog," "on little cat feet."

ℒistening

> Listen carefully, my (child), to the master's
>   instructions
> and attend to them with the ear of your
>   heart.

ST. BENEDICT

St. Benedict, in founding his order of monks in 480 C.E., set up a rule for living which provided order, continuity, and routine for monastic living. He begins the prologue to his Rule with the above quotation. His very first admonition tells us to *listen*.

Listen is the key word here. I have a difficult time letting go of activity and sitting in silence to listen. My worth as an individual is deeply predicated on the amount of work I do. I may have been brought up in a Catholic household, but several generations in a pluralistic society has pounded the Protestant work ethic into my family psyche.

Actually God has been trying to get his message of listening across to human beings for many centuries. Even when Moses was leading them out of Egypt, God complained about the hard hearts of the Israelites, the hearts that would not listen. Generations of prophets were sent. Jeremiah tried to warn them that God was unhappy with their worship of others gods. In an oracle to the people he said: "Listen to my voice" (Jer 29:20); "I will be your God and you shall be my people" (Jer 31:22). Samuel admonished Saul: "Listen to the message of the Lord" (1 Sm 15:1b). Isaiah, in his first servant oracle, begins with: "Hear me, O coastlands, listen, O distant peoples" (Is 49:1). Jesus too, leaving the disciples and crowds of people, went off by himself to listen and hear what his Father had to say.

All this emphasis on listening sent me to my prayer space and the word that emerged was, You *have to change!* Joan Chittister tells a Sufi story about change which helped me to take the plunge into a new way of prayer. "How shall we ever change, the disciples asked, if we have no goals." And the master said, "Change that is real is change that is not willed. *Face reality and unwilled change will happen*" (italics mine).

This last sentence surfaced in my thoughts for the next several days. Facing reality showed me that I am slowing down physically, unable to work from sunup to sundown as I had done when I was younger. I had a whole new series of needs including a great longing for simplicity and a deep desire to become closer to my Creator.

Finally I spent several prayer times taking a good, honest look at how I had prayed as an adolescent, young adult, middle-aged mother, and now a grandmother. It became evident that very often, especially when moving from one stage of development to another, my prayer life had changed. I had not always prayed in the same ways; I had adapted my prayer life to my needs of the moment. Sr. Ann Chester, IHM, calls them "sea changes of mind, heart, and spirit" as we grow older. Although I had been comfortable in my prayers during these last years, God was showing me that instead of talking to God with words, it was time to listen and hear his words. I had to relinquish control of how I prayed, trusting and finding faith that God would show me the best way.

Good friends do not carry on one-sided conversations; they give their full attention to the other. Using Basil Pennington, Macrina Wiederkehr, Thomas Merton and many other spiritual writers, I am learning to sit in solitude and silence with my closest friend, Jesus, listening and hearing as well as talking. Being open and honest in my part of the dialogue deepens our relationship.

St. Augustine's prayer has become my prayer: "Our hearts are restless, O God, until they rest in you."

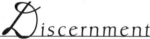
Discernment

> *Your will be done, on*
> *earth as it is in heaven.*

How many times have I repeated the Lord's Prayer,
day after day, week after week? Yet I slide over that
phrase, *your will be done*, without a thought or even a
question of its meaning or what it is that I am saying.
"Your will be done." How do I know what God's will
is?

I don't think I worried much about "God's will"
when the nuns at school tried to instill that concept
into us. It wasn't until after my husband Jim died
that I finally came to the realization that God and I

had to be partners or I would never get through the next twenty years. These days, the gentle urgings of Benedictine spirituality have cemented "Your will be done" into my psyche. Slowly my frozen heart is thawing into a beating, loving "heart of flesh."

Benedict begins his Holy Rule with "Listen carefully." Later on he says "the Lord reveals." This leaves us in a quandary. How do we listen when there are no audible words? If God reveals, how do we know it? Some of us rely on church pronouncements; some of us are sure that our thoughts on a subject are God speaking to us. Yet the truth lies somewhere between those two extremes, often including both, yet taking in so much more.

The strange thing is that we find God's will in very ordinary ways. He shows us constantly which way to go. If we train ourselves to understand his words then we can find the grace and love which bring contentment and peace to our journey. If our minds are closed, if we are not open and aware of promptings, then we go on our own merry (and sometimes not so merry) way, wandering far from what God, in his infinite wisdom, knows is best for us.

How can we thaw out those frozen hearts and hear God's words? Certainly they do not always come as they did to St. Paul, a flash from heaven that knocks us off our horse. Nor do they always come as a feeling from within us, although sometimes they do. How do we know?

The first step is to pray each day for the ability to understand God's words in whatever form they come. Often his words come through a book, a magazine, or a newspaper I am reading. Sometimes a statement made on television or the radio will cause an "Ah, ha!" moment. Most frequently, a comment from a friend or acquaintance will be the trigger. My morning, evening, and night prayer, in which I join in the prayers of all Benedictines, can also be a time when I hear God's whisper in my ear.

But sometimes God has to hit me on the head. Take last week for an example.

The past few weeks have been a time when I questioned my ability to write, a time when I could find just about any other job to do, except to go to the computer and sit there until some words came out. Procrastination was my middle name, even though that still, small voice within said: "Get to work, Cathy. You have a gift. Use it."

I was still vacillating when the mail brought a letter from England, five hand-written pages from a man who wanted to thank me for my book *When Your Parent Dies*. A deep depression after his father's death had led him on a trip to the west of Ireland where he chanced upon my book at Our Lady of Knock Shrine. It brought him out of the depths of despair and back to his family and work, knowing he could deal with his grief. My writing was God speaking to him.

That was not the end, however. That same week I got a phone call from Kentucky. It was almost as if God didn't trust me to let the one message push me off the starting block. A young man whose mother had just lost her husband was mailing *When Your Spouse Dies* to her that day. She was overwhelmed with grief, wondering how she could ever go on. Would I consider calling or writing her? Again he thanked me for writing the book. I also received this message. Michael's letter from halfway around the world and the one from Kentucky were both God's voice: "Here you are, Cathy. Keep writing." I had prayed for an ability to see God's will, and I saw.

So here I am this morning, writing to you about prayer and discernment. When I sat down I no idea what I would say. Yet an hour later, I have written several pages. There will be revisions, rewrites, and changes, but basically, I have been used as a channel of God's will—a very humbling experience. Just be open to God's word and you will know.

God's Will

Upon my bed at night
I sought him whom my soul loves;
I sought him, but found him not;
I called him, but he gave no
*   answer. . . .*
Do not stir up or awaken love until it
*   is ready.*

SONG OF SONGS 3:1, 5B

During the last Christmas season I read Solomon's Song of Songs and it remained in my heart and mind even until now. I try so hard to find God's love, yet it remains elusive. Solomon knew. Love comes when it is ready, not when I think I am ready. God knows when it is "the fullness of time" much better than I.

After Jim died I begged and pleaded with God to send me a love, a husband who would walk with me through the years as we raised those nine children and found our way to the God who made us. But no one came. There was no answer to that prayer. I suppose you could assume that God said no. He had other plans and I had a lot to learn.

C.S. Lewis says that the danger in needing love from a human being is that we give too much love to the human and at the same time, withdraw that love from the God who made us. It is not that human love is wrong but rather that it is often out of proportion to the love of God. If God had sent me a husband to love when I asked, would I ever have been open to God's love as I am today? Perhaps God's plan was to show that his love would be more than enough.

I may be aware of my penchant for directing my own life in many ways, but God always has a few surprises and tends to confuse me. My need for love was real, but God had different ideas about it.

I had a lot to learn about following God's will. Jesus' prayer, "Not what I want, Father, but what you want," is the prayer that brings me back where I belong. The little phrase, "What would Jesus do?" gradually allowed me to step back and become aware of my drive to find love in a man. Slowly but surely, with prayer, reading, and spiritual direction, I am learning to accept God's will, to let go of the control which I had deemed so necessary. Today, in a different form, his gift of love is the delight of my life.

Blindness

> When they arrived at Bethsaida,
> [some people] brought to him a blind
> man and begged him to touch him. . . .
> Putting spittle on his eyes he laid his
> hands on him. . . . Then Jesus laid
> hands on his eyes . . . and he could
> see everything distinctly.

MARK 8:22-25

I want the touch of Jesus that I may see! His touch heals in stages. I saw—as in an ancient mirror—when Jesus touched me the first time at my Cursillo, and it opened my heart to seeing God's word in a new and different way. I never would be the same after that weekend. Now I am asking God to again touch me and sharpen my vision.

Spittle on my eyes was somewhat revolting to this twentieth-century child, but I am beginning to see the earthiness of Jesus' healing. In the beginning we were made from clay. We need the moisture of the earth to patch our cracks—and we have so many of those. What could be better than the moisture from Jesus' lips? When I was a child, my mother spit on her hankie and cleaned my face almost automatically. She was determined that others would see me as a clean, loved, and well cared for child. Jesus too was showing the people of Bethsaida that not only did God love and care for this blind man, but he is also our loving and caring Abba, our daddy.

Do I really recognize God's touch? A Jesuit poet has verbalized our experience:

Thou mastering me
God! Giver of breath and bread. . . .
And dost thou touch me afresh?
Over again I feel thy finger and find thee.

GERARD MANLEY HOPKINS
"THE WRECK OF THE DEUTSCHLAND"

God's hand is always on my shoulder if only I am open to it.

Truth, Secrets, and Freedom

"You will know the truth, and the truth will set you free."

JOHN 8:32

Truth. What is the truth? What is true for one is not always true for another. What is truth for me as a child is not the truth as I move into old age. What is wrong with "little, white lies" that make our relationships and days go a little easier? Is there a freedom—no matter how painful—to knowing the truth?

The word *truth* covers a wide variety of similar terms all having to do with accuracy and honesty. We look at the words reality, actuality, sincerity, integrity, and fidelity to a standard, and say: *In reality, if I told my friend the truth, it would turn her life upside down, so everyone will be better off if I don't tell her.* We all skirt around the truth or omit it entirely in order not to cause pain in others. Yet how many times is someone hurt when a truth is withheld over the months or years? Many painful topics have to be faced some time or another, even when it hurts. Family secrets such as pregnancy before marriage, adoption, drug or alcohol abuse by a parent or relative, child and spousal abuse, or mental illness are often withheld from children, even though everyone else knows about it.

Even Pontius Pilate had trouble with the meaning of truth. In John's gospel Jesus tells Pilate "The reason I came into the world is to testify to the truth. Anyone committed to the truth hears my voice." Pilate's retort, "Truth! What does that mean?" showed the confusion in the ruler's mind.

Yet deep down, most of us know when truth is required. Mother's old adage, "What does your conscience tell you?" spoke the truth. Josh Billings, the American humorist, said it well: "Reason often makes mistakes, but conscience never does."

Thomas Merton wrote: "The lie brings violence and disorder into our nature itself." How do we find the courage to face the truth, to bring a peace and serenity into our lives instead of violence and disorder, even when our fear of hearing the truth seems too great?

I have found that turning to face my fear, yes, sometimes even embracing it, turns the giant into a paper midget. However, I can't find the courage to hug my fear of the consequences of truth without God's grace. Sometimes all I can do is to pray: *Lord, I want to tell the truth, I want to be open about what happened. Please help me!*

Finding the courage to admit our own faults and imperfections, or even the failings of our siblings, spouse, parents, or grandparents takes time. If we can be open with others, we will also be teaching younger generations. Most of the time teaching comes, not from preaching or telling, but from example. This is one of the most important roles for older people.

A few years before she died, my aunt told me that her parents ran away to get married in the 1890s because my grandmother had been pregnant. I had grown up hearing the stories of my "saintly" and lovable grandmother, who surely couldn't have ever done anything wrong!

I learned from that story, however. She and my Catholic grandfather had turned their very human failing into an impetus for growth. When the baby died at birth, the couple "had their marriage blessed" (as we used to say) and eventually Rosaltha became a practicing Catholic. It was not easy for my aunt to tell this story, but, by their action, Rosaltha and

Jerry had taught their grandchildren and great-grandchildren how to rise from a sin and form a loving, honest relationship.

Honesty often means practicing "tough love," primarily with myself, but sometimes also with my loved ones. In the long run the result is harmony, freedom, and peace within myself and my relationships. Serenity is worth the risk.

Answering the Call

Yahweh . . . called, "Samuel, Samuel!"
Samuel answered: "Speak, Yahweh;
for your servant is listening."

1 SAMUEL 3:10

"Cathleen, Cathleen!" How often have I answered when the Lord called me? Was I too busy or too tired to answer? Was it really the Lord calling me? Does he always break in on my sleep to tell me something or ask me to make a dramatic life change?

No, of course not, although he could speak in that way.

God does sometimes speak to me in that light alpha sleep which produces dreams. But most of the time his word comes through someone else: my spiritual director, a good friend, my sister, holy scripture, or the priest as he gives a homily at the eucharist. Sometimes his word comes through my reading, though not always in a "God book" as my young son used to call a spirituality book. A well-written novel, a biography, or a memoir can trigger a memory or a hidden message that is God's way of showing me the way.

Often a TV program, a movie, a video, a beautiful piece of music, or an artist's painting will have a profound effect on me, allowing me to hear God's voice entering my inmost heart. A walk outside on a crisp fall night with a harvest moon glowing through the leaves still left on the cottonwoods and oaks can be God saying: "See the beauty I have given you. Enjoy!"

Can I, with Samuel, say: "Speak, for your servant is listening?" I pray to have the grace that will show my eagerness to please my Creator. When I am loved and I love in return, our mutual affection will affect others and make the world a better place.

Death

> "Now, Master, you can dismiss your
> servant in peace; you have fulfilled
> your word. . . ."

LUKE 2:29

Simeon was an old man who had prayed all his life, asking God to let him see the Messiah. His was a prayer of letting go; he was ready to die now that his prayer had been answered.

    Looking at my own death is a scary thing, even though intellectually I know it is part of life. In today's world we have lost touch with its immediacy and inevitability. This wasn't true for my mother's generation. She remembered listening to the sound of an uncle building a casket for her dying grandmother while she, a eight-year-old girl, lay in her bedroom wondering what was going on. Grandma Magdalena had lived with the family for many years and their mutual love was an important part of Loretta's life. As the little girl wondered about the commotion, her father picked her up out of bed and brought her to the bedside where all the aunts and uncles were standing. The tiny woman with a white night cap tied under her chin smiled at her, held her hand and said goodbye to the granddaughter she loved so much. Then Loretta was put back into bed. Eighty-five years later this scene was as vivid as the day it happened.

Death was a part of life in the early 1900s. Today we do not experience this aspect of living. Death is something we see on the TV screen, read about in the newspaper, or encounter in the funeral home. We hide it in hospitals and hospices, only attempting to explain it to ourselves and our children by euphemisms: "She is gone . . . sleeping . . . away . . . she was in so much pain . . . so old. . . ." As a consequence, we have built up a fear of death. Writers and psychologists call us a death-denying society. We fear what we do not know.

Everyone dies. According the psychologists if we are afraid of something, the only way to cure that fear is to turn and face it, not ignore it, run from it, or cover it up with busyness. In order to rid myself of the fear of death I need to acknowledge that I too will die, reaffirming my faith—or perhaps finding it for the first time—that there is a life after death.

I need to go in prayer to the bedside of my parents and ancestors, hold their hands and acknowledge that I have been afraid to look at this fear, rationalizing that if I ignore it, it would miraculously go away. I must ask those ancestors to help me to find the faith to say: "Your death was a part of your life— and mine. My death is a part of my life—and my children's."

Lord, help me to accept not only life, but the death that leads to new life.

We will die; we also will rise again just as Christ has promised. It may take the rest of our life to realize this, but if we repeat these words from the Our Father, perhaps the mystery will gradually take hold of us: "Your kingdom come; your will be done."

Our search for faith, our belief that there is life after death in the kingdom of God, the kingdom come as we have prayed for so many years. When we say "Your will be done," we acknowledge that God will choose the time and place of our death. As we come to realize the truth of these phrases, we will be ready to pray Simeon's prayer:

Now, Master, you can dismiss your servant in peace; you have fulfilled your word.

The Blessing Prayer

May Almighty God bless you,

the Father, the Son and the Holy Spirit.

THE LITURGY OF THE EUCHARIST

At the end of the Sunday liturgy the priest raises his hands and says: "Bow your heads and pray for God's blessing," then repeats the blessing above. Last Sunday I wondered: *Do we ever take this ritual and make it part of our family prayer time?* Most of us are so rushed we find very little time for praying together. But a brief blessing prayer can easily put us into

God's presence as we begin our day at work, home, or school.

> God bless you and keep you in the palm of
> his hand
> In the daytime and night-time, on sea and
> on land;
> In sadness and gladness, in joy and in woe,
> God bless you and keep you wherever you
> go.

BRIAN O'HIGGINS

The word *blessing* comes from the Latin *benedicere*, to speak good of someone. Psychologists point out the need that children and adults have for affirmation, a positive statement of approval or judgment. A blessing, however, is more than an affirmation. A blessing calls down God's overwhelming love and care on our loved one.

When we visit a sick friend or relative and leave them with a blessing prayer, those words linger on until our next visit. We are leaving them in God's care.

> May God bless you with strength, accep-
> tance, wisdom, and knowledge.
> May his words heal both spirit and body.

Tracing a cross on the forehead of our spouse, child, or grandchild as they leave for their daily school or work, we might say:

> May the Lord keep watch between you and
> me when we are out of each other's sight.

GENESIS 31:49

Or, with a little more time, pray:

The Lord bless you and keep you;
the Lord let his face shine upon you,
and be gracious to you;
the Lord look upon you kindly and give
you peace.

NUMBERS 6:24-26

We can remind a teenager leaving for semester tests or a spouse leaving for a tense day at the office that God's peace and inspiration through his saints will help them through the day ahead. They are not walking alone.

May St. Thomas Aquinas (or your patron saint) be with you as you call on them today.

A blessing doesn't have to be long; if we are running late, it might be a quick hug and the prayer:

May God hold you in the palm of his hand.

What special action has your child done recently or what special quality do you admire in them? Why not use that for your blessing some morning?

Lisa, you have really shown God's love to the new girl in your class by making her welcome in your crowd. May you always be a channel of God's love, and may the Lord of Life be always with you.

We are all beloved sons and daughters of our Father. How about repeating the words that God said about his son?

You are my beloved son (or daughter), on
you my favor rests.

MARK 1:11

We might use Isaac's blessing to his son, Jacob,
when we wish success in a new venture to a son,
daughter, or friend:

May God give to you of the dew of heaven
and of the fatness of the earth
and much grain and wine.

GENESIS 27:28

There is a one-word Hindu blessing commonly
used in India on meeting or parting from an acquaintance or loved one, "Namaste." It means:

I honor the place in you where the entire
universe resides;
I honor the place in you of love, of light, of
truth, of peace.
I honor the place within you where,
if you are in that place in you and I am in
that place in me,
There is only one of us.

RAM DASS, GRIST FOR THE MILL

Surely, if families bless each other as they leave
home for school or work, not only are they individu-
ally blessed, but so are the communities in which
they live and work. God promised Abraham:

I will bless those who bless you. . . .
all the communities of the earth
shall find blessing in you.

GENESIS 12:3

When the Lord called Abraham he made a promise that would continue for generation upon generation. How great it would be if we took advantage of this blessing.

I can't say I do it all the time, but I'm trying! If each of us blessed one person each day, what a difference we could make in the world!